Alternative
Therapies
For Horses

ALTERNATIVE THERAPIES FOR HORSES

Vanessa Britton

WARD LOCK

A WARD LOCK BOOK

First paperback edition 1995

First published in the UK 1995
by Ward Lock
Wellington House
125 Strand
LONDON
WC2R 0BB

An imprint of the Cassell Group

Distributed in the United States
by Sterling Publishing Co., Inc.
387 Park Avenue South, New York, NY 10016-8810

Distributed in Australia
by Capricorn Link (Australia) Pty Ltd
2/13 Carrington Road, Castle Hill NSW 2154

A British Library Cataloguing in Publication Data block for
this book may be obtained from the British Library

ISBN 0-7063-7449-5

Typeset by Litho Link Ltd, Welshpool, Powys, Wales
Printed and bound in Great Britain by Bath Press

This book is not intended as a substitute for the medical
advice of veterinarians. The reader is advised to consult a
veterinarian regularly in matters relating to his or her
horses's health.

CONTENTS

This book is dedicated to all those equestrian enthusiasts –
whether they are a weekly rider, an owner of ten horses or a
veterinary surgeon – who are courageous enough to keep an
open mind when all those around are cynical.

ACKNOWLEDGEMENTS

Horse health is a subject which creates great emotion amongst horse owners and health care specialists alike. In writing this book I consulted many specialists. Some could not have been more helpful and answered all of my questions patiently and knowledgeably. Others seemed to view my questions with suspicion – perhaps they were worried about what I was going to include in this book! I hope that when those specialists read this book their fears will be reversed, for it is my sole intention to promote awareness of their treatments. Throughout the chapters, the need to consult a specialist in a particular area has been stated.

For those who offered freely their time and knowledge I am extremely grateful. These include: Tony Howe for giving his expert knowledge of swimming horses so readily; Stan Harding for taking the unprecedented step of coming to visit the author, and Tony Gilmore for reading the text, both of whom are skilled chiropractors of the highest merit; Melanie Gurdon, a very highly respected animal physiotherapist, for making me so welcome at her home and for allowing me to tag along on her calls, taking photographs; Sherry Scott for sending such helpful information and reading the text and Sharon Kerr for sending her very interesting information; John Nicol for his advice on acupuncture; Warwick and Chris Townsend of Feedmark for their help with the herbal section; Pauline Ferrie for her invaluable practical advice about treadmills; Colin Roberts, MRCVS, for his technical advice about the use of treadmills for diagnosis and research; Chris Slater of Surrey Treadmills; Wendy King for (as always) never minding about the disruption my photography sessions cause to her stable routine; Christine Dunnet for help with some of the photographs; and my Editors, Alison Goff and Jane Birch – for being so patient!

Thanks also to Sara Wyche for her enthusiasm and helpful suggestions on the text.

All photographs by the author except for those on page 70, which are reproduced by kind permission of Stan Harding, MC, AMC, MIPC, and those on pages 78 and 80 by kind permission of John Nicol, MRCVS. Line illustrations are by Rodney Paull and Mike Shoebridge.

FOREWORD

Social and economic factors such as increased leisure time, improved income, and the availability of relatively inexpensive livery facilities close to urban areas have led to the enormous rise in popularity of horse riding. It is also supposed that sitting on the back of a horse simply enables people to enjoy fresh air and the countryside without particular exertion.

However, for most horses and riders hacking out is only a small part of the overall routine. Far from being an activity without physical effort, most riders actually seek to increase their experience of the horse's movements far beyond the three basic gaits of walk, trot and canter.

Horses are kept as part of a sporting heritage, mainly by those living in an industrialized society. Here, technology has created an environment which requires only the minimum of physical involvement. Whether driving a car, operating machines, or watching TV, it's a largely sedentary existence. Yet movement is an important part of our self-expression as human beings. The rhythm of our movements makes us identifiable as individuals. We revitalize the often depleted sense of our own natural state through the movements of another being – that is why we ride horses.

Today's riders no longer simply subscribe to age-old traditions of horse keeping, and horses are no longer judged on their economic merits alone. In rekindling a sensitivity towards ourselves, we have perhaps become all the more discerning towards our horses. This has led many horse owners to explore the possibilities of alternative therapies, in the hope of finding healing with quality, therapeutics without side effects, and above all, personal participation in the whole healing process. In the absence of adequate reference material on alternative therapies, there will probably have been many disappointments.

This book gives a comprehensive description of the alternative therapies available to the horse owner. It acknowledges the expertise of those professionally trained to put them into practice, but it also emphasizes the resources available to every horse owner: namely their own hands, eyes and commonsense. Above all, and thank goodness, it reminds us that the basis for every successful therapy is a sound diagnosis.

Sara F. Wyche MRCVS

INTRODUCTION

More and more horse owners are turning to alternative therapies and complementary medicines, which not so long ago were dismissed by many as mysterious modern fads. It is true that technology is increasingly playing a large part in the training of horses. Fitness programmes are now including the use of treadmills and swimming, for example, but many complementary treatments have been around for thousands of years, and at one time some were the only form of medicine available.

Some horse owners have turned to complementary medicine as a last resort, when conventional treatments have failed. Others have an alternative therapist, whether it be a homoeopath or an acupuncturist, who visits regularly to help cure a variety of disorders and keep their horse generally fit and well. Complementary therapies are still viewed with suspicion by many horse owners and conventional veterinary surgeons and are often regarded as 'cranky'. However, some veterinary surgeons are more open-minded and in response to demands from the equestrian population are starting to think about referring certain individual cases to the complementary therapist.

TRADITION VS TECHNOLOGY

In years gone by there were only two options open to horse owners when their horses became ill. Either they tried to treat the horse as best they could themselves (and this may have been by using herbs and homoeopathic remedies) or they called in the veterinary surgeon. Veterinary treatment was considered to be expensive and often horses would suffer

for fear of large bills which horse owners knew they would not be able to pay. Thankfully most horse owners now seek expert assistance when needed and worry about the expense later.

There are now many more options open to owners concerning horse fitness and health. Technology has moved into the equestrian world and owners are able to call upon the knowledge of healthcare professionals in their quest to produce healthy equine athletes for each and every discipline. The owner is able to feel part of a team which employs a totally holistic approach. In the past owners may have felt excluded by veterinary surgeons who failed to explain what they were doing and simply issued instructions on how to manage a certain condition. There may have been no thought given to the practicalities of carrying out such instructions, and as a result horse owners often became bewildered and disillusioned.

Getting a horse back to full fitness takes a lot of skill and a 'team' approach. The vet gives a diagnosis, the specialist provides the means of repair and rehabilitation, the owner provides the tender loving care and the horse behaves himself!

To derive the most benefit from this book, keep an open mind and consider the benefits of each therapy in the light of individual circumstances and individual horses. There is no right or wrong, there is simply what is right for you and your horse. Whatever the scientific arguments, if a certain treatment relieves a horse's condition then it is a valuable therapy.

While you can learn how to use herbs or massage to the benefit of your horse's well-being, a veterinary surgeon should always be consulted if your horse has some form of illness. Alternative therapies are complementary to conventional treatments and only where alternative therapists are also qualified veterinary surgeons may they work to the total exclusion of conventional medicine. The alternative therapist will accept the diagnosis made by the veterinary surgeon and will then use the evidence of personal observations to select the most appropriate therapy for the horse. The layman should feel no more able to carry out the healthcare professional's job than the veterinary surgeon's.

Whatever individual prejudices there may be with regard to treating horses, the fact is that there is a revival in natural therapies. The important thing to realize is that all complementary therapies harmonize with each other: they do not compete. In many cases a horse may be receiving treatment from two or more specialists – a homoeopath and an acupuncturist for example.

The interest in equine physiology and sports therapy has snowballed in recent years and the need for experienced equine sports therapists has now been confirmed. Not only will they play a large part in helping performance horses to reach their full potential, but they will also form a bond between themselves, the vet, the owner and the horse, helping each combination to maintain health and fitness at the appropriate level.

Equine therapy is a vast subject. No book can hope to cover the complete range in great depth but the aim of this book is to make horse owners more aware of just what alternative fitness training methods and complementary therapies are available. Using this new knowledge, owners can contact a specialist in the field which they feel will suit themselves and their horses best. However, they should also bear in mind that, while one form of therapy may suit one horse, it will not necessarily suit another. Horses are all individuals and a great deal of flexibility is vital when considering alternative fitness training or complementary therapy.

1 Keep your Horse Healthy

Health and fitness are not aspects of horse management exclusive to top competition horses; nor are they only within the scope of the top professional trainers and riders. Through correct care, you can ensure that your horse is healthy and by putting in a little effort you can attain a level of fitness that is suitable for your chosen activity, whether it be eventing or simply hacking. All horses have their own limitations, governed by such factors as age, health and breeding, but they should be able to attain levels of health and fitness appropriate for their lifestyle and the work they are capable of doing.

By ensuring correct feeding and management you ensure a healthy horse, but there are no set rules to getting it right and sometimes, through no fault of your own, your horse may become ill, or be injured. Obviously, you will want to try and achieve a quick recovery so that your horse suffers minimal pain and you can both get back to work as soon as possible.

The Healthy Horse

There are certain signs which will tell you if your horse is generally in good health. The healthy horse is bright, attentive and in good body condition. His coat will have a nice sheen and he will generally look fit and well. There are also physical checks that you can carry out to satisfy yourself that all is well:

- **Eyes** should be bright and focused. On turning the eyelids outward you should be able to see a nice salmon-pink membrane.
- **Nostrils** should be moist, and they too should be a nice salmon pink colour inside. There should be no thick, yellowish discharges.
- **Limbs** should be free from excessive heat or swelling. When your horse is trotted up he should put weight evenly on all four feet and strides should all be of a uniform length.
- **Skin** should be supple and easy to rock back and forth on top of underlying layers. Your horse should feel warm and dry to the touch and his coat should lie flat against his skin. If you pinch the skin it should immediately spring back into place once released. If the pinch of skin remains visible then he is showing signs of dehydration.
- **Appetite** is usually one of the first things to be affected when a horse is feeling ill.

Signs of Ill Health

Generally the sick horse will appear listless. He may hang his head and let his ears droop. He may look to be tucked up with his tummy pulled in, and he might even seem unsteady on his feet. Physical signs of ill health include:

- **Eye membranes** changing colour. Pale membranes might indicate that your horse is suffering from anaemia, chronic indigestion or worms. Deep red membranes are a sign that he may be running a fever, whereas red membranes with a blue tinge indicate pneumonia. Yellow membranes might indicate a disorder of the liver and blue-red membranes are indicative of heart and circulatory problems.
- **The coat** may appear to be standing on end or 'staring' and dull in appearance. This is often the case in malnourished horses. If the mane is easily pulled out this might also indicate ill health.

Horses need plenty of freedom from the stable.

• **The skin** gives several warning signs about different conditions. Generally the skin of a horse in ill health will tighten up. Your horse may be in the early stages of a general disease; he may have lice or be generally malnourished.

• **Sweating** also indicates problems. While excessive sweating may be caused by too much exercise if your horse is unfit or by nervousness or excitement, these should be familiar to you. If on the other hand your horse breaks out into a sudden cold sweat he may be in acute physical pain or suffering from some form of mental imbalance. An uncharacteristic hot sweat is often a clear indication that your horse has a fever.

• **Limbs**, if puffy or swollen, denote ill health. If the puffiness is due to a bone or joint problem your horse will almost certainly be lame. If the limbs are generally puffy, your horse might be suffering from heart trouble or a digestive problem. Localized puffiness may indicate a skin irritation or condition.

MAINTAINING GOOD HEALTH

We all know the saying 'prevention is better than cure' and this is very true when managing your horse's health: prevention, in the form of basic general hygiene, is cheap, while cure may run to hundreds of pounds in veterinary bills.

• A horse should receive a balanced diet relating to exercise, size and metabolism, and should always be provided with clean water.

- A horse should receive basic routine care such as regular worming, vaccinations, foot care and dentistry. According to individual situations, horses will need worming every six to eight weeks. Vaccination takes place once a year after the initial course has been administered. Rasping of the teeth should be done once a year, although the younger or older horse may need more regular attention. Most horses need shoeing every five to six weeks while in work. Those out of work need trimming about every eight weeks.
- A horse should always be allowed plenty of freedom from the stable and be turned out as much as possible. If horses must be kept in for any period, they need plenty of walks in-hand as their mental state will soon affect their health if they are shut in all day.

Such routine care can prevent health disorders. The healthy horse is less likely to succumb to disease, infection or injury, and the extra time spent attending to such detail is a small price to pay for peace of mind.

When Things Go Wrong

Knowing your horse is the best preventive treatment. If you really know him, his likes, dislikes and little foibles, you will instantly know if something is not quite right.

Having identified a problem, the first step is to have a veterinary surgeon diagnose the ailment. You then have to decide whether you want your horse treated conventionally (usually by the use of drugs) or by alternative methods, such as those described throughout this book. Both have their own merits, and in a broad sense can complement each other if the specialists involved work well together. There are times when conventional treatment, such as surgery, is the only option; but there are also times when alternative medicine can offer the most appropriate solution. The biggest problem, for any horse owner, is finding a veterinary surgeon who also practises complementary medicine such as homoeopathy or acupuncture, or one who will refer your horse to a specialist.

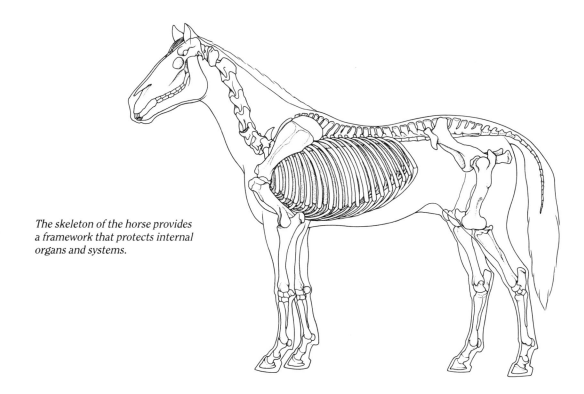

The skeleton of the horse provides a framework that protects internal organs and systems.

Physiology

While maintaining health is a good starting point, if you expect a horse to do consistently well in competitions, you also need to consider how your demands will affect him. Endeavour to learn a little about horse physiology and how the bodily systems are involved in health, fitness and performance. This will help you to recognize when something is wrong, or more importantly when something is about to go wrong. Those systems are:

● the **musculoskeletal system** which provides the propulsive force;

● the **cardiovascular and respiratory systems** which together provide the raw materials to motivate the muscles;

● the **nervous system** which coordinates the whole activity.

The aim of training is to maximize the capacity of each of these systems, usually by gradually and progressively burdening them so that the system adapts to cope with the increased demand.

The musculoskeletal system

The musculoskeletal system is made up of bones, joints, ligaments, muscles and tendons, each having different needs and so requiring different management. This means that all cannot be totally satisfied by any specific training system: there needs to be a compromise.

The **bones** provide a framework which protects internal organs and systems. This framework is an active and energetic system which is capable of an adaptive response to external stimuli. The structure of bone tolerates great strength and is able, by virtue of a certain amount of elasticity, to sustain the stresses of tension and compression. This means that while a bone can be snapped by too great a force acting upon it sideways, such as hitting it against a brick wall, it will endure far more pressure if the force is applied from top to bottom, such as when landing over a show-jump. It is also designed to adapt to mild strain, which results in increased bone density. Bone strain is less at the walk, slow trot and canter, so ideally it is these gaits which need to be

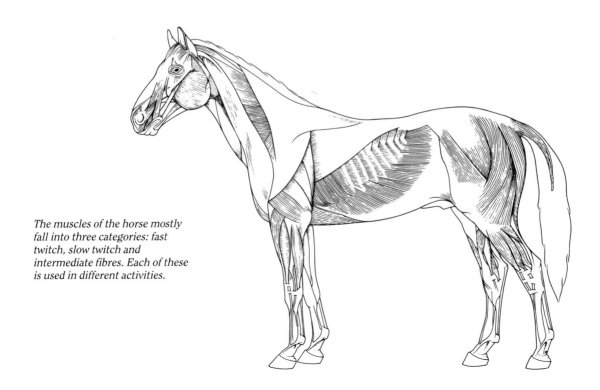

The muscles of the horse mostly fall into three categories: fast twitch, slow twitch and intermediate fibres. Each of these is used in different activities.

employed when aiming to stimulate bone development in your horse.

Joints are the junctions between two or more bones. The majority afford movement between the bones, although some have no movement. Their main purpose is to assist and restrict movement between the opposing bones.

Ligaments also help to support the bones. Their purpose is to restrict the joint movement to a normal range. If the joint overbends, the ligament becomes overstretched resulting in strain. Strained ligaments take considerable time to recover and will lead to insecurity of the joint as they do not regain their former state.

There are various types of **muscle**: those that are required for movement of bone are known as skeletal muscle; that which controls the heart is the cardiac muscle and there are also those which form the internal organs. Generally, muscles fall into three categories: fast twitch, slow twitch and intermediate fibres. **Fast twitch** fibres contract rapidly and powerfully but quickly become exhausted. They are capable of generating a large amount of energy but for only a short time. In contrast, slow twitch fibres produce relatively little tension and contraction is slow, but they are very resistant to fatigue. Slow twitch fibres need oxygen to function well – this is known as functioning aerobically. Fast twitch fibres can function in the absence of oxygen and this is known as anaerobic functioning. Consequently, slow twitch fibres are ideal for endurance, best utilized by long-distance horses and eventers, and fast twitch fibres are for speed and power, most useful for the show-jumper or sprinter. The point at which the muscular system changes over from anaerobic metabolism to aerobic metabolism is called the **anaerobic threshold** and muscle is best trained by working at this level. It starts to become clear that the objectives of training the show-jumper or sprinter are different from those for the endurance horse or eventer.

Tendons extend from the base of their respective muscles and connect to various parts of the legs and feet. They have a very high tensile strength and as a result can endure great pressure. They have four very important responsibilities to carry out. Firstly,

Fast twitch fibres, capable of generating a large amount of energy but only for a short space of time, are utilized by the horse when taking off over a jump.

they act as shock absorbers to any sudden force and as a back-up when tired muscles can no longer take the strain. Secondly, they act as an elastic energy reserve; when pressure is put on the limb they 'give' and store energy from the force of impact, then when the leg leaves the ground they recoil and give the limb an elastic thrust which does not incur the use of any energy. Thirdly, during swift muscle contraction they will act as a booster; and lastly, they are responsible for conveying muscle activity to the bones.

A tendon must be able to stretch and relax if it is to act as a shock absorber. The tendon is highly at risk when muscles are tired: the muscle no longer takes the strain and the tendon must do so instead. This is when tendon injuries occur. It is extremely important to condition the muscles correctly to avoid such unnecessary strain and then to condition the tendons during early fitness training to provide optimum elasticity.

Cardiovascular system

The cardiovascular system is concerned with the heart and blood vessels. It operates in order to deliver oxygen to the muscles quickly, which aids aerobic energy production. The amount of blood delivered to the tissues varies with rest and exercise. During exercise the blood supply to the muscles is dramatically increased. The horse will need to increase the uptake of oxygen to supply the demand of the increased blood to the muscles and also because the heart rate will increase as a result of the exercise.

Respiratory system

The respiratory system is responsible for the presence of air within the lungs which is then ready for collection by the blood to distribute to the tissues. The rate of respiration is governed by exercise. At rest the horse breathes steadily without effort. During periods of exertion respiration rises in order to supply enough oxygen to the system.

Nervous system

The nervous system is responsible for ensuring that all parts of the body communicate and are controlled by the brain. Some of the functions are activated by conscious effort; others happen as a result of automatic response.

The nervous system also acts in self-preservation. 'Shut off' occurs when horses have reached the limit of their capabilities and this is commonly known as 'heart'. The horse who shuts off near the limit of capability is said to have a big 'heart', one who shuts off well before the limit has a small 'heart'.

Additionally, the nervous system controls reaction time. As this is partly inherited, the progeny of a quick athletic horse are sought after. Quick reactions can also be taught, however, and the intelligent horse soon learns that an uninterrupted order of muscle stimulation leads to economy of effort. Therefore the horse also learns to suppress undesired muscle activity.

Allowing Personality to Develop

When developing horses for performance there is a danger of forgetting they are individuals, not machines. Their personalities must be allowed to develop alongside their physical abilities and at no time should we forget that we can only train horses because they allow us to do so. If we have to try to force the horse, we have gone wrong somewhere along the line.

The horse's mental attitude is very important as we need a willing, cooperative partner to be successful in competition. A kind and cheerful temperament is a great asset and we must work hard to preserve such an outlook. The work regime should be varied as much as possible by combining schooling sessions with hacks and in-hand work. A horse should also be allowed plenty of freedom in the field with other companions. It cannot be stressed enough that all horses are individuals and this must be taken into account before the correct regime can be found.

Involving a Veterinary Surgeon

It is a sound practice to involve a veterinary surgeon in health care from the moment you acquire your horse. A good initial overhaul may pay dividends later on as you will know your horse's strengths and weaknesses and will be able to take them into account when devising fitness training and health-care plans.

After that, it is a good idea to ask for a check-over on every veterinary visit (when the vet is giving your horse vaccinations or rasping teeth, for example) as problems can creep up unnoticed.

Prevention is always better than cure, but it is impossible to prevent something unless you have an indication that it is about to occur. Early detection is more likely if your horse is checked regularly. It could prevent him from being out of action for a long time, which might be the result of a problem going unnoticed until it has exploded.

The equine physiotherapist

Recent scientific knowledge has changed the way many injuries and illnesses are treated. For example, the traditional way of treating tendon breakdown was to fire or blister them, but this has now been recognized as ineffective. Modern complementary therapies such as ultrasound and laser (Chapter 5) have proved to be far more beneficial and, having diagnosed a problem, the veterinary surgeon will very often prescribe such treatment to be administered by an animal physiotherapist.

When and why to look for an alternative

Many horse owners are concerned about keeping their horses on drugs for long periods, especially as ruling bodies have banned the use of many of the effective drugs.

Complementary therapies and alternative treat-ments are now enjoying a great revival as horse owners come to realize their many benefits and varied use. Many alternatives are available to the horse owner and not just those which concern treatment of injury. For example, there are alter-native fitness training methods with the aid of treadmills and swimming pools (Chapters 3 and 4). These can be a great help when a horse goes stale and needs a new environment and work schedule for a while, as they will help to maintain the animal's fitness until traditional work can be resumed.

Taking a hand in the recovery of your horse after illness or injury and keeping him healthy afterwards can put a whole new perspective on future care. You may decide to incorporate herbs into the diet and use massage to soothe away aches and pains. You may also find that a regular check-up from a chiropractor or a homoeopath may be a beneficial form of preventive health care.

Keeping a horse fit and healthy is a challenge. There are no definite answers about which training method or therapy is the best one as every situation and individual horse poses a different problem. However, with correct veterinary diagnosis and the skills of complementary healthcare professionals, you can have the best of both worlds.

The holistic approach

One of the attractions of alternative or complemen-tary healthcare is holism, which is a widespread philosophy common to most alternative therapies. The idea of holism is not a new one and if thought about carefully makes a great deal of sense. The concept of a holistic approach is that a body cannot be reduced to a collection of parts. There is a strong spiritual emphasis behind any treatment and the horse is seen as a spiritual as well as a physical and emotional being within a particular environment. In order to help the horse in times of illness, he must be taken as a whole. Viewing the body as an inseparable structure, with a tendency towards health, is important to all the natural healing techniques, whose job it is to support and correct dysfunction in a basically sound system so that it may return itself to normal.

Those who employ a holistic approach when treating horses believe that the horse has an innate intelligence, which will, given the right circum-stances, help the body to heal itself. To many this is a hard concept to understand and is perhaps best summed up in the words of B. J. Palmer, discoverer of chiropractic and founder of the Palmer School of Chiropractic: 'You cannot treat the body without affecting the mind and spirit.'

2 KEEP YOUR HORSE FIT

WHAT IS FITNESS?

Essentially, fitness is the capability of the body to function more effectively. When horses are relatively unfit their bodies will be working quite lethargically and they will tire quickly. As fitness increases, heart and lung (cardiovascular) capacity will increase, resulting in the body working more efficiently for longer periods, and so they will tire far less quickly. However, horses can only be expected to attain appropriate levels of fitness for competitive disciplines if they are healthy and well fed. Many of the horses that receive alternative therapy are competition horses. Generally this is because they are under constant pressure to perform and the stress on their limbs and body is great. Often the problem is clear – a sprained tendon or a cut, for instance – and this is where a physiotherapist may be able to help. Frequently there are no visible signs to illness but you can sense that your horse is just not right: this is where a homoeopath or acupuncturist may be able to help. Of course many therapies overlap, and horses with an injury may also have some underlying problem which caused them to falter and hurt themselves in the first place. There are no hard and fast rules as to what therapy will help a certain condition, but the aim is to keep the horse fit and healthy so that there is no need for treatment anyway.

There is no secret formula which will tell you when your horse is fit for a given purpose but there are various methods of fitness training. As long as you stick to the method you have chosen and are careful to observe your horse's progress, you will succeed in achieving the desired level of fitness, though you may have to adapt the routine slightly to suit the individual's mental and physical state.

The horse's body can be burdened by other influences and it is important to take all other contributing factors into account. These include:
● **Rider fitness:** Unfit riders tire horses quickly, as they will have to carry passengers rather than partners.
● **Health:** any form of illness or injury will hinder the ability of the horse's body to function efficiently, so that any form of work takes more effort than normal.
● **Nutrition:** if the horse's nutritional needs are not correctly met for the workload, bodily requirements will not be replenished at the necessary rate for optimum functioning. This often results in some form of deficiency and in turn may affect health.
● **Conformation:** a horse with poor conformation may have to put in more effort to achieve the same results as a horse with good conformation.

Any physical effort uses energy, which is discharged through the muscles. As you work your horse over a period of time, the activity of the heart and lungs is increased to replace the energy that is being used. Lactic acid builds up in the horse's system as this energy is used up. Muscles will lose their elasticity and begin to ache if this acid is not removed and recycled by oxygen in the blood. If this does not happen properly, an excess of lactic acid builds up and the muscles will tire to such an extent that they will be liable to injury.

The fit horse's heart and lungs pump the blood carrying oxygen efficiently through the system to

The fit horse's heart and lungs are able to work at maximum capacity.

the muscles, and are able to work at maximum capacity. There is then enough oxygen present to convert the lactic acid back into energy (in the form of glycogen). Where there is insufficient circulation of oxygen to the muscles they will tire, leaving the horse vulnerable to serious injury as the stress is then taken by the tendons and ligaments. A typical example of this is when the hunter who has been turned out all week without being ridden, is suddenly expected to do a full day's hunting at the weekend.

Fitness does not just happen by chance. A programme needs to be worked out which will develop your horse's potential to perform well in your chosen sphere. To do this the programme must aim to develop the horse's qualities:

● **Athletic ability**, by means of gymnastic exercises over poles and grids.
● **Stamina**, by following a clearly defined training pattern so that the horse does not become unnecessarily fatigued at any point.
● **Ability to utilize own suppleness and balance**, to carry the rider more easily and manage energy levels more effectively.
● **Response to the aids** – an obedient, trustful horse conserves energy by complying; an uncooperative horse expends energy by fighting the rider.

The aim is that, at the peak of fitness, horses will be able to perform to the best of their ability. Such horses will be able to perform more consistently for a longer period as they will always be working within their limits. The responsible owner will recognize this and plan a suitable programme for the sphere of equestrianism in which the horse will be required to perform.

INDICATORS OF FITNESS

Before deciding upon any training programme you should ensure that your horse is fit and healthy. It is impossible to gauge how well your horse is doing if you have no idea of initial fitness and without an initial assessment it will be more difficult to recognize if he is less than healthy throughout the training programme. To do this you need to take some initial readings of your horse's temperature,

pulse and respiration rates while at rest (this is referred to as '**measuring the TPR**'). Additionally, you need to be aware of your horse's everyday health. Preventive, alternative healthcare also has a role here and many of the therapies discussed in the following chapters can be used as preventive measures, to ensure the horse's fitness throughout the competition season.

TPR should be measured before work, while the horse is resting. It is important to take the readings at the same time each day so that a picture can be obtained of what constitutes 'normal' for your horse. The normal TPR rates for a horse at rest are given in Table 1, with an indication of how they will rise during exercise.

TABLE 1: NORMAL TPR RATES			
	at rest	steady exercise	hard exercise
Temperature (°C)	37.5–38	38–39	39–40
Pulse (beats per minute)	35–40	40–115	115–200
Respiration (breaths per minute)	8–15	40–70	70–100

MONITORING FITNESS

Monitoring your horse's fitness will take the guesswork out of whether the programme you have devised is working well or not. Readings of your horse's temperature, pulse and respiration rates during periods of work will help you to build a picture of progression. At first, the TPR will rise quickly and take time to revert to normal with only steady exercise, but as your horse becomes fitter the TPR will remain constant for longer periods before rising and will also recover more quickly.

Taking the TPR rates

Taking a horse's temperature is fairly straightforward as long as you are well prepared. Shake the mercury down so that is it well below 37°C, then lubricate the bulb with petroleum jelly. Lift the horse's tail and, standing to one side, insert the thermometer into the horse's rectum about half way, at a slight downward angle, and leave it there for at least one minute, ensuring that you hold the end securely. Remove the thermometer and read immediately.

The pulse at rest is usually taken by feeling the maxillary artery where it crosses the jaw, or alternatively with a stethoscope over the heart on the horse's near side, just behind the elbow. Count the number of beats per 30 seconds and multiply by two to get a reading per minute. When monitoring during exercise it is easier to take a count for 15 seconds and multiply by four to find the rate per minute, as most horses are fidgety and will not stand still for 30 seconds.

Whilst mounted, during exercise, the respiration rate can be counted by watching the horse's flank move in and out (one in-and-out movement equals one breath). When unmounted, the easiest way to

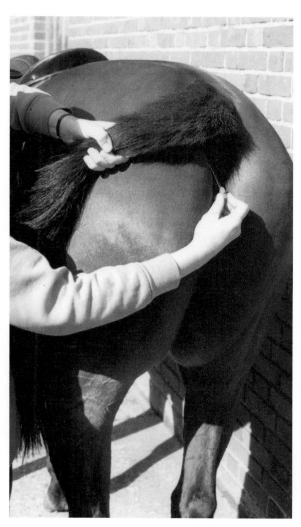

Taking the horse's temperature.

The pulse at rest is usually taken by feeling the maxillary artery where it crosses the jaw.

The pulse can also be felt just behind the horse's elbow on the near side.

check the rate is to place a hand over the nostril and simply count the breaths felt, which at rest should be even and regular.

Blood tests

Blood tests can also be beneficial in monitoring fitness but first a horse's 'normal' blood profile must be known. A blood test will show the amounts of certain components within the blood. Each of the components which make up the horse's blood have been isolated and assigned a range which constitutes normal. On analysis, any deviation from these 'normal' values will indicate illness, thus offering a strong recommendation not to compete in an event at a given time.

FITNESS TRAINING METHODS

The basic method of training horses has not altered much over hundreds of years and has always been considered more an art than a technical skill. However, many trainers now take advantage of scientifically designed conditioning programmes which often use treadmills or swimming as an integral part of training.

Trainers use different methods to achieve fitness and each will be slanted towards the individual horse's specific area of ability, whether it be racing or show-jumping. Some trainers take advantage of scientific advancements; others stick to tried and tested methods. Whatever method is employed, the primary aim of any fitness regime is the same: to delay the onset of fatigue to an increasing degree as the horse's fitness improves. The horse which performs consistently well is the one which best maintains speed and rhythm and only a horse who is not fatigued can do this.

The method you choose needs to suit your individual circumstances, your limits on time and your facilities. It is pointless to employ a method which you cannot hope to stick to as this will only end in failure and disappointment.

Contrasting competitive spheres make differing demands on the horse and so the demand on energy production will vary. The horse needs to be exposed to the types of stresses which are familiar to a particular competitive area. The aim is to expose the horse for the shortest amount of time required for adaptation to take place.

There are three phases of training common to all fitness methods: conditioning, fitness training and fitness maintenance.

Conditioning

Conditioning is the term used in the equestrian world for pre-fitness work. It is an extremely important part of any fitness programme and it is here where later problems can be prevented. Essentially it is a period of slow work, walking and then trotting with a variation in activities and exercises, which takes about six weeks to accomplish. It starts with walk periods of 30 minutes per day, building up to around two hours towards the end of the conditioning period.

Conditioning is an essential requirement to any fitness programme and the basic aim is to impose enough stress to produce adaptation to cope with the stress, but always without overstressing the horse. It is a period where the horse's musculo-skeletal and circulatory systems will be toned to produce a response which will utilize nutrition to its maximum benefit.

One of the spin-offs of conditioning is that the horse is afforded time to adapt mentally. A youngster will learn to enjoy being ridden and a novice horse will learn to be calm when away from the stables. The psychological impact is great. Anxiety is reduced and the newcomer is helped to accept what may seem to be an unfamiliar and curious development.

Fitness training

Traditional methods of fitness training simply use periods of exertion repeated systematically, with the aim of building the horse's resistance. This is a little hit-and-miss and does not give any real information on improvement, which could easily lead to over-stressing of the system. It is difficult to know if the horse is coping with the planned work regime until a problem occurs, and then it may be too late to put it right. Any form of training can only succeed if the rider (trainer) knows how far and how fast the horse is actually working.

Interval training

Interval training follows a far more logical method and is often used by event riders who need their horses to be super-fit to cope with the demands of the discipline. It alternates periods of exertion (usually a set canter/gallop) with periods of rest during which the heart and lungs are permitted to recover partially before being stressed again. This steadily increases the recovery capacity of the heart and lungs by building up their strength gradually and systematically, enabling the replacement of energy to be accomplished in the shortest time.

Monitoring of the TPR provides a precise check on the state of recovery, so that the workload can be adjusted to suit the individual horse. While the horse recovers at the expected rates, the training can progress steadily. However, should the time for recovery show that the horse is not coping and is being overstressed, the workload must be reduced until the recovery rate improves.

Lengthened recovery times may also be due to other factors, such as the humidity, inclement weather conditions, rough terrain or excessive speed, so you need to discount these before deciding your horse is not coping.

Fitness maintenance

Fitness training is time-consuming. It comes as a great relief then to realize that, once the fitness target has been reached, the level of fitness can be maintained in most horses by working only three or four times a week. Many riders are under the misapprehension that their horse will become even fitter if they continue with the pressure and the hard work. In fact this is the quickest way of sending the horse over the top, resulting in loss of enthusiasm and even injuries. Having reached peak performance a horse's system needs a chance to let down or else no adaptation takes place and the body does not cope as well.

No horse can be kept fit in this way indefinitely, however, and there will come a point when fitness starts to drop. If the training programme has been devised well, this will be at the end of the season. Thus the aim of any training is to condition the horse early in the season so that fitness training can begin in plenty of time to reach peak performance around the time of competition. Fitness maintenance then carries the horse through the competitive season. Fitness starts to drop near the end of the season when the horse is ready to be turned away.

THE STRESSES AND STRAINS OF COMPETITION

Whichever fitness method is employed, there will come a time when the horse is fit enough to move into work specially suited to his discipline. This will be at different stages for the various disciplines, on what can be visualized as a ladder of fitness. The show horse only needs to reach the first or second rung before branching off into specialized training, whereas the eventer needs to reach rung five or six before beginning specific training. The three phases of training remain constant, however. Once a horse has completed the conditioning period and has done sufficient work for the level of fitness required, the task is to maintain the horse without losing condition or going over the top and becoming stale.

Each discipline has its own specific stresses and strains but most horses learn to cope if properly prepared. There is an element of 'keeping the horse sweet', though. Maintaining enthusiasm over the competitive season is demanding for the trainer and takes skill. Careful monitoring of the horse's mental attitude is just as important as the physical checks.

There are several indications of well-being:
- Good nature and a relaxed outlook
- A relaxed stance at rest, but without any signs of resting a forelimb
- Alert and showing interest when approached
- Appetite remaining good.

Signs of staleness include:
- A change in personality
- Loss of appetite, which may indicate the onset of an illness or loss of enthusiasm
- Resentment of work – a sure sign of staleness
- Uncharacteristic unwillingness to travel – the horse does not want to 'perform' any more.

Poor performance

To cope with the stresses of competing, travelling and training, performance horses make great demands on their diets. They need a higher intake of high-energy foods, minerals and supplements to sustain their bodily needs during the season. Poor performance is one indication that those needs are not being met. There are many other contributing factors to poor performance but the ones owners dread are injury and illness, as very often these cannot be prevented and are hard to control.

What are the options?

While all is going well there is no need to look to an alternative form of training. But what if things do go wrong? Traditionally, horses that go sour, get injured or lose performance are put out in the field for six months' rest. However, this is often unnecessary. The saying that a change is as good as a rest is particularly true with horses. They are often expected to do the same work day in, day out, without any thought being given to their outlook on life. In the wild, horses roam around, their environ-ment changing all the time. We can never simulate this type of environment totally, but we can partially satisfy a horse's requirement for change by offering alternative forms of exercise.

There are alternatives to traditional training. For the conditioning period, you might consider slow walking exercise on the treadmill or in a horse walker. To build up fitness you could complement ridden work with a programme of swimming or treadmill work and the same equipment can also maintain fitness. However, you should not view such equipment as a lazy way of getting or keeping your horse fit. There are no easy options and it is all about selecting equipment that will complement your horse's training and then adapting its benefits to your best advantage. The concept of holism should also be borne in mind. Together with a suitable fitness programme you should consider the benefits of preventive healthcare; your horse may benefit from the use of herbs or preventive chiropractic, for instance. Remember that alternative therapies all complement each other but success lies in finding which combination suits your particular horse best.

Contrasting competitive spheres make differing demands on the horse.

3 THE TREADMILL

A treadmill is a piece of equipment on which to keep a horse moving at a certain speed, without covering any ground. There are high powered fixed units and there are portable models. Generally the more high-powered the unit, the faster the horse can travel – up to full galloping speed. The width of the treadmill allows a horse to walk in and stand comfortably but it is not wide enough for turning around. The floor is a non-slip revolving belt which can be regulated to different speeds, depending on whether the operator wants the horse to walk or trot, and so on. Many treadmills have an incline as well as speed controls and can be set to achieve the maximum benefit for an individual horse, in as natural a way as possible. Fixed models allow the horse to walk straight through from one end and out at the other, except that a bar at chest height stops the horse from travelling forwards when the treadmill is in use. One of the drawbacks of some portable models is that the horse has to be backed off because they are built as a three-sided cage with only the back open.

USES FOR TREADMILLS

The most obvious purpose of a treadmill is to exercise a horse when it cannot be ridden, but treadmills also have many therapeutic benefits. They might be used to keep injured horses in work, or

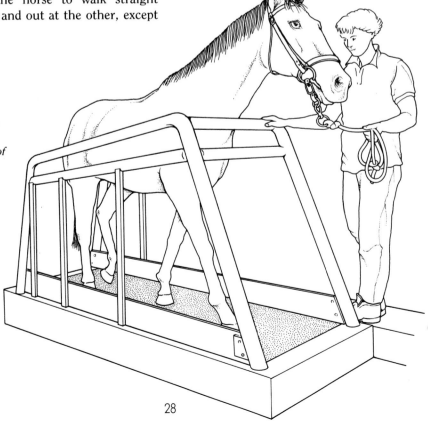

The type of portable treadmill machine installed by many horse owners. It aims to provide even use of muscles from head to tail.

help to rehabilitate horses after illness or injury, under veterinary supervision.

The main benefit of a treadmill over traditional forms of exercise is that horses can be exercised straight, without the stress of a rider and without being on the turn, as they would be when lunged or on a horse walker. The most obvious use then, is for back conditions – the horse can be exercised without a rider. The non-slip surface provides minimum concussion on the limbs, especially where the floor has been cushioned as an extra safeguard. This allows the limbs, joints and muscles of the legs and back to be worked without jarring or rider pressure, whereas otherwise the horse would probably have to be rested.

The exercise can be built up gradually and calmly, which helps to prevent the breakdown of a healing injury. This is one benefit over ridden exercise at such a time, as horses recovering from injury often want to let off their pent-up energy and decide a good buck or two and a jog up the road will suffice, only to find that their leg hurts once again when they stop!

For monitoring recovery

The treadmill can provide valuable information on the stage of recovery. When a horse is recovering from a back problem, there are always worries about whether there is some other complication such as the saddle pinching, or the rider not sitting straight. But when a horse is worked without anything on his back there is no doubt – either he is showing signs of pain or he is not.

For monitoring viral conditions

The treadmill is useful when determining whether a horse is over any viral condition he may have had. It is difficult to diagnose such conditions at rest, but the controlled environment of the treadmill allows an accurate diagnosis to be made. Viral conditions often have an effect upon respiration and the heart and, as the treadmill produces cardiovascular exertion, it is possible for the veterinary surgeon to see whether the horse is breathing and coping with the exertion as expected or not.

CASE HISTORIES

ICE KING: 15.2 hh grey gelding, 13 years old. Show-jumper. This horse had been sweating up under the saddle in an unusual way. Firstly he was swum, and then he was put on the treadmill. A heart-rate monitor was used at all times to see if his heart rate was abnormal at any time.

It took a week to train him to walk, trot and canter on the treadmill, yet his heart was normal at all times. It became obvious that the horse was only receiving pain when saddled and ridden; whatever the problem, by eliminating rider and saddle the sweating was also eliminated. He had a fortnight of swimming and treadmill training and then returned to his owner (who had altered the saddle) without a recurrence of the problem.

BLUE PETER: This big backward 2-year-old racehorse had both respiratory and back problems. He was sent to a therapy centre to have swimming and treadmill sessions. He started swimming, but because of his breathing difficulties he did not cope very well and a decision was made to concentrate on treadmill work.

He began with a gentle, 15-minute walk, morning and afternoon, progressing through a fortnight to brisk walking one hour in the morning and the same in the afternoon. It was clearly visible that the muscles in his back had started to work properly and he was a lot happier in himself. He went on to complete his racing career without recurrence of the initial problems.

For foreleg problems

Horses with some form of foreleg problem may get relief from working on an incline at slow paces, for the weight is largely taken on to the hindquarters as when trotting uphill out on a hack. However, it is thought that too much work on a steep incline may cause injury to the hocks, as the horse cannot find his own pace to cope with the stress but is forced to maintain the speed of the moving floor. Such exercise needs to be closely monitored.

For problems with gait

Where horses have problems with gait, treadmills can be used to re-educate their movement. As the floor can be set at a rate that suits an individual pace, so it can be set to make a horse achieve a desired pace. A horse which comes up short, for example, can be persuaded to stride out. Unrestricted movement can be observed while standing behind and in front of the horse, although this should be done with caution as shoes have been known to fly off.

For highly strung horses

Many horses work themselves up into a state of anxiety when exercised on the heath or out hacking. Because the treadmill gives repetitive exercise it seems to have a calming effect.

For monitoring and improving fitness

Treadmills can be used as fitness aids, although they are not designed to take the place of conventional exercise. A horse being worked in canter and gallop on a treadmill could be got very fit but would still need to complete training out on normal exercise, if only to keep mentally happy. Ideally, treadmills in the fitness setting would be used to complement rather than replace ridden exercise. For instance, they can be used to maintain fitness when injury or bad weather conditions prevent other forms of exercise.

When using the treadmill solely as a fitness aid a routine can be planned so that the level of fitness that should be obtained can be calculated. Equipment such as heart rate monitors help to record such levels. As a fitness aid, a treadmill can save

CASE HISTORIES

PENNY: 17.1 hh, Hanovarian, 7 years old, dressage horse. This mare had competed well for two seasons, then she started to come up short on her near hind when asked to lengthen. On examination a problem was found with the near hind hoof. The wall of the hoof was contracted, so that the hoof was at least an inch smaller than the off hind. The muscles of the hindquarters were also very tight, resulting in unbalanced movement.

Firstly, the mare received attention from an orthopaedic farrier to promote correct hoof growth. Then she underwent a period of remedial exercise on the water treadmill to help improve the muscle condition. She progressed slowly at first, until the hoof started to regrow normally, when the improvement was dramatic. She has since returned to work competing in dressage as previously, and novice BHS eventing.

MORGAN: 15 hh stallion, 7 years old. This horse was used for showing in a trap. He had an injury to his leg and had been rested. His owner wanted him to go on the treadmill so that she could be absolutely sure that he was sound and in no pain, before showing him again.

He was put on the treadmill in walk at first, until his confidence showed the handler that he was ready to trot. When he was trotted he was completely sound. He was walked and trotted on the flat and on an incline for a week. His own veterinary surgeon came to observe him while on the treadmill and pronounced the horse fit to resume showing.

A treadmill can be used to determine problems with gait.

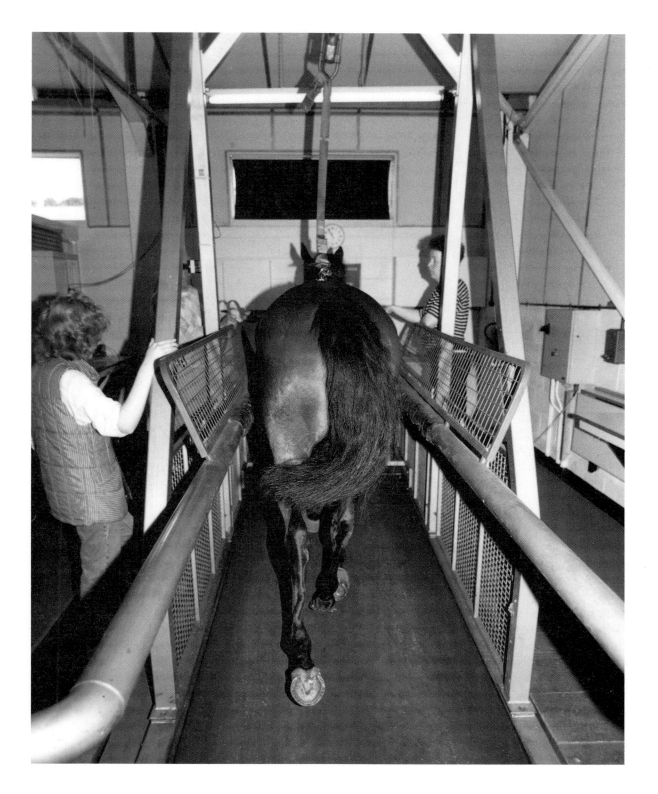

much time and money. For example, the horse who needs one and half hours of road work can take equivalent exercise on a treadmill in only 30 minutes at a working walk. The time can be increased according to the individual horse's needs. Work on the treadmill should be alternated with other ridden or in-hand work, for both correct development and mental fitness, so a total training plan can be devised. The greatest advantage of treadmills is that they allow the horse to work with the least amount of concussion. The greatest disadvantage is that the muscles that the treadmill works are not necessarily those that would be normally exercised with traditional ridden work.

Some of those owners who have them use their treadmills to warm up before exercise, or to walk horses with (or prone to) colic. Some yards in the USA and Scandinavia use treadmills solely as a fitness tool for competition horses, while others use them to get yearlings fit for sales. In the majority of cases, and as long as they are correctly introduced, these youngsters seem to accept the treadmill quite readily. It is something different and seems to satisfy their inquisitive and playful nature, provided that it is not overdone. The danger when training yearlings is that too much stress will be put on their still developing joints. However, as long as the machine is set to match the youngster's strides, they can improve fitness and help to develop a good strong back and hindquarters. This is actually a benefit when it comes to backing, as the youngster's frame is physically better developed, which lessens the likelihood of strain on the limbs. Ordinarily most youngsters are lunged to prepare them for further work or the sales. Lungeing is thought to put unnecessary strain on a youngster's limbs, so a treadmill in this setting provides the benefit of always working on a natural straight line.

For initial conditioning

The treadmill is an ideal machine for starting a horse on his initial conditioning programme. When a horse first comes up from grass he is likely to be overweight and so the treadmill can provide the early walking exercise without the concussive effect often produced by road work.

OPERATING A TREADMILL

Operating a treadmill may look easy but there are risks, especially on high-powered models. Slower models, advertised in the equestrian press, are aimed at owners who perhaps do not have as much time to ride as they would like and these are becoming more popular, but it is important to gain experience and learn how to use one properly before jumping in to such a venture. Concentration and common sense must be combined with technical knowledge about the machine.

Experienced operators are totally confident about working the machine and in turn the horses learn to have confidence in them. Generally, high-powered models should only be used by experienced operators, but most owners can learn how to use a basic yard model safely. Unfortunately some owners put horses on treadmills and leave them unattended for the exercise period, which is both dangerous and reckless; imagine what would happen if the horse stumbled and there was no one about to switch the machine off quickly. A treadmill must be monitored at all times by a competent operator.

As a safety precaution horses usually wear front brushing or tendon boots and overreach boots when on the treadmill and also a safety harness on the high-powered models. The harness would catch a horse that stumbles and would automatically switch off the machine.

Introducing the horse to a treadmill

The first lesson is used as an introduction to the treadmill and should be kept fairly short. The horse is allowed to have a good look at the machine and is then walked through a few times until he is relaxed and happy. If the model requires the horse to back off, then ensure that your horse will back up on command before entering the unit. A bar is put across the front of walk-through models; the horse is quietly walked up to the bar and the machine is then switched on at slow walking pace. The feel of the floor moving underneath does feel a little odd to a horse experiencing it for the first time and so it is very important to reassure him with the voice. Once the horse realizes what is happening, he soon settles

The horse is quietly walked up to a bar across the front of the treadmill before the machine is switched on at a slow walking pace.

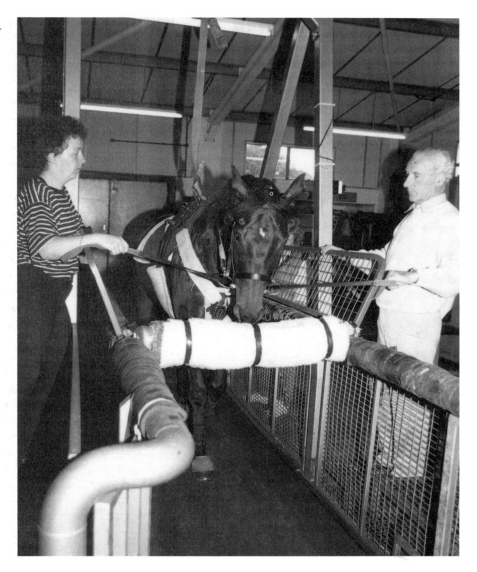

into a nice rhythm. Give a gentle build-up over a period of days until the horse is working in a nice relaxed outline.

At first, the speed of the machine is matched to the horse's natural pace. Some dressage horses or those with a long striding action will need the pace set faster than a shorter-striding animal, so that they are not stressed at any time. It is important not to frighten them in any way. With experience, it is easy to see if the horse is not comfortable at any pace and the speed can be adjusted accordingly.

The horse is encouraged by voice to walk on, trot on or canter – voice control is as important as in any other discipline. Experienced operators will know the exact moment when a horse should break into a different pace and can give encouragement if he fails to respond to the speed.

Once the horse is quite happy on the treadmill a programme of exercise can begin, building up to cantering and even galloping if this is required. However, the horse must be confident at the slow paces before being asked to go any faster or uphill.

Types of Treadmill

The machine most used by horse owners is the walking machine with a fixed floor angle (usually about 6 degrees) which aims to provide even use of muscles from head to tail. Most allow the speed to be varied from a standstill up to 6.5 km (4 miles) per hour. The machine can be set to suit the specific stride of the individual horse.

A slightly more sophisticated machine allows both walking and trotting, up to about 11 mph. This machine can help in further fitness work along the lines of interval training. The horse is walked to warm up, then trotted for a given length of time, allowed to recover partially and then trotted again. Built in speedometer, mileometer and stop watch are aids to monitoring exercise. These machines are increasingly seen in eventing yards.

The more high-powered models are too expensive for the average horse owner and need experienced operation, but some centres do take in outside horses for fitness and rehabilitation work on this equipment. The floor angle can often be varied on these models as can the speed up to galloping pace. It is therefore possible to overwork the horse in a very short space of time – hence the need for experienced operators.

Underwater treadmills

These machines are finding favour in racing circles for pre-race and post-race exercise, and in some therapy centres. They can provide alternative exercise as the horse has to work quite hard to pull the legs through the water; however, they should only be used as a means to an end, not as an integral part of a training pattern.

By their very nature underwater treadmills have two opposing effects. The water makes it harder for the horse to lift the limbs forward while at the same time the moving floor actually takes the limbs backwards.

Close supervision is extremely important as it is harder for the horse to maintain a natural rhythm due to the extra effort required and so the machine must be set accordingly and altered in line with the horse's effort.

These machines do not have a floor angle, but the depth of water can be varied from a couple of inches up to buoyancy. They are beneficial in a therapy setting (under veterinary supervision) for treating leg problems, because a buoyant horse is working with minimal weight and concussion on the legs. Many models have built-in jacuzzi jets which can be set at various angles, to massage either the lower or upper limbs as desired.

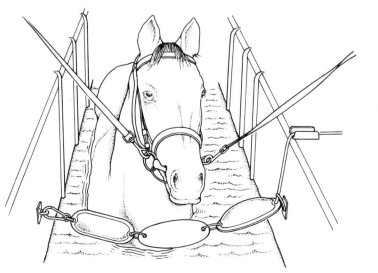

An underwater treadmill.

THE TREADMILL AS A DIAGNOSTIC AND RESEARCH AID

The advantages of a treadmill in the diagnostic or research setting is twofold. Firstly, by having a treadmill in a controlled environment, standardized exercise tests can be run. Competition training is so 'high tech' these days that it is important to ensure that horses can cope with the training regimes put upon them. By using a treadmill, horses can be strenuously tested in safe laboratory conditions, to test how their bodies endure and adapt to such exercise. The aim of such tests is to understand more about how horses work and so to be able to advise on how best to minimize the stress of work.

Research centres which use treadmills are able to study normal and abnormal responses to exercise and in particular the effects of exercise on the heart and lungs. In tests, a fit horse is put on the treadmill and connected to apparatus that measures breathing, blood pressure and body temperature, first at rest and then progressively through walking, trotting, cantering and galloping. This helps to build a picture of how horses will stand up to the stresses and strains of high performance. The horse will often wear a lightweight face mask over the nostrils to measure the speed and gas composition of air flow, giving a breath by breath account.

The temperature and humidity in the treadmill building can be controlled; the track surface is constant, as are the speed and the time at a given speed. Wind speed is controlled with the use of fans, so that a test done in the middle of summer is comparable to one done in winter.

The second advantage is that a horse can be travelling up to 49 kph (30 mph) – 44 kph (27 mph) is normal Grand National speed – without covering any ground. This enables the taking of measurements which would be impossible out in the field at that speed: even if blood and air flow tests were taken from a horse which had just pulled up from a good gallop, there would already have been a lot of changes and so it would not truly represent the exercise.

It is the veterinary surgeon's job to monitor clinical trials, but the operation of the treadmill is left to an experienced operator who makes sure that there are two handlers holding and a driver as well, so that the horse does not get a chance to drift back.

Should there be any problem – for instance the horse becoming unexpectedly fatigued – there is an emergency stop button. If this is used, the horse is able to stop dead, from 12 m (yd) per second, in approximately 3–4 seconds. Some centres fit foam cushioning over the metal plate so that it is less concussive to the horse's legs.

The treadmill controls enable the operator to measure speed in metres per second: 1 metre per second is 2.25 miles per hour; 1.6 m/s is normal walking speed on a treadmill; 8.5 m/s is novice BHS event speed; 10.5 m/s is Badminton phase D speed and 12 m/s is Grand National speed.

It is clear that the study of horses on the treadmill benefits those training on it and those who go on to high performance, but what does the future hold? Will we be reducing the stress our horses have to cope with in competition, or will we be developing a race of elite equine athletes?

4 HYDROTHERAPY

Hydrotherapy is a means of healing the horse by using water. The physical properties of water can be used to treat certain conditions or maintain health. There are various ways of engaging water to benefit health and these include: swimming pool, jacuzzi, water treadmill, water walks or simply by hosing or walking through a stream.

SWIMMING

Swimming a horse is a fairly straightforward process. Whether you are swimming for health reasons, or as part of a fitness programme, you simply take your horse to an equine pool and let the experienced staff take over. Where your horse has a health problem, you should have your veterinary surgeon advise on the suitability of swimming for the condition, but for fitness maintenance the staff at the pool will be able to offer expert guidance on suitable exercise programmes.

How does a horse swim?

A horse used to swimming will move through the water in an extended trot, which is, of course, a two-time diagonal movement. Such an experienced swimmer will give maximum extension, with most of the power coming from the hindquarters. However, the effort required to make this movement is equivalent to that of a canter, which is why swimming is more strenuous than an extended trot on the flat.

Horses find the activity very tiring and are in danger of quickly becoming fatigued while being introduced to swimming, which is why only experienced handlers should swim horses.

When horses are first introduced to swimming, they may initially move in a more haphazard canter movement, often described as a doggy-paddle, until they learn to relax and attain the trot movement. Horses are natural swimmers but some accept the activity more readily than others.

A horse used to swimming will move through the water in an extended trot style movement but the effort required is equivalent to that of a canter.

The main advantage of swimming is that it provides weightless exercise.

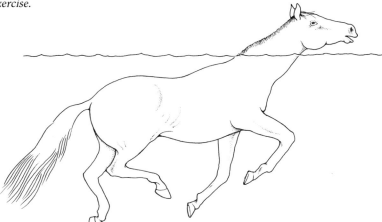

When first introduced to swimming, a horse may adopt a haphazard 'doggy-paddle' style.

Swimming with your horse

Cantering along the seashore has become very popular. Many people box their horse to the beach simply to provide a change to normal hacking routes, while others go for the therapeutic benefits of the sea. If while riding along the seashore you suddenly find you have wandered out deeper than you thought, you may unexpectedly find your horse swimming underneath you. If this happens you should remember to keep in the centre of balance. Although a horse is capable of swimming with you on his back, if you were to slip backwards towards his quarters he will be severely hampered in his thrusting movement from the quarters, which is essential if he is to stay afloat.

It is a sensible precaution to fit a neck strap if you intend to swim, as the horse's head must always be free when swimming. It is also wise to put on tendon and overreach boots to prevent injury. Above all you should ensure that you keep parallel with the shore-line just a few lengths from where the horse can reach the bottom. Should the horse tire unexpectedly you can encourage him to take those couple of lengths to safety relatively easily. The sensible rider will only swim for short periods at a time so that such a situation does not occur.

The benefits of swimming

The main advantage of swimming is that the buoyancy factor of the water drastically reduces the force of gravity. This provides weightless exercise, which enables injured horses (who under normal circumstances would have to be rested) to carry on full exercise without having to put any strain on an injured part. The recovery process is therefore considerably speeded up. While buoyant in the water, a horse is affected by an upward force known as hydrostatic pressure. This is increased or decreased in relation to the density and depth of the water. This pressure, aided by the cohesive property of water, helps the horse to massage the injured parts by having to pull his own weight through the water, against the pressure.

Other benefits of swimming include:
- keeping horses which have just been gelded clean and helping to relieve any resulting stiffness;
- keeping down swelling;
- helping tendon or joint injuries;
- monitoring viral conditions;
- recovery of hoof conditions;
- recovery of pulled muscles;
- recovery of sore shins;
- diagnosis and recovery of back problems;
- recovery of sprains and wounds.

Swimming is an activity that can be divided into two clearly defined areas: remedial therapy and fitness training (hydroexercise). The benefits for each are many and varied.

REMEDIAL SWIMMING

For joint or muscle problems

Traditionally, rest is indicated when a horse has a joint or muscle problem, as any weight on the limbs may exacerbate the condition. Swimming provides an alternative to rest in such cases. As it is weightless exercise, the limbs can move freely through the water with less pain than there might otherwise be. The joints and muscles can be kept active: if left immobile they would only deteriorate.

For recovery from injury

After an injury some horses are cautious about using the injured part. However, once they are in the swimming pool they seem to forget the injury and swim well. This is partly because they have to use the full movement of their joints in order to swim and partly because any friction of the joints is reduced underwater. The water exerts an even pressure on the limbs which in turn helps to increase and maintain good circulation.

In many cases, a horse will overcompensate for an injured limb by putting too much pressure on the opposite uninjured limb. The uninjured limb is then in danger of being strained. In the pool, the horse does not have to put weight on the painful leg and will swim with an equal force from both legs, thus maintaining an even body development. Chronically injured horses have been known to swim for a period of 12 months, at the end of which time you would never know that they had not been cantering.

CASE HISTORIES

HOLLIE: 15 hh, chestnut mare, 5-year-old hunter. While jumping a fence out hunting this mare fell into a ditch and became trapped. One of her shoulder joints suffered severe damage to the muscles. This led to extreme muscle wastage to the extent that the bones of the shoulder could easily be seen and the joint would dislocate easily. Initially she received physiotherapy to help relieve the pain and encourage the recovery process, but the shoulder was still very unstable.

Swimming was seen as the last resort as the horse was under threat of being put down and the owners were very concerned. Muscle development was the desired outcome and so the mare, after a controlled build-up, was swum 10–12 circuits of a round pool very strongly each day. On re-examination the shoulder had become much more stable and the muscles were developing normally, becoming much stronger. Swimming continued for a month, when the muscles had built up enough for the mare to be turned out daily. From then on she rapidly improved and went on to be ridden by the master of the local hunt.

BLACKIE: 15 hh black gelding, 7 years old. This horse fractured a splint bone in a point-to-point race. His trainer wanted box rest kept to a minimum as he knew that the horse's muscles would start to waste if he was kept rested. Swimming was ideal for this type of injury, as it provided weightless exercise.

Three or four weeks after the injury occurred the horse's vet was happy that he could be transported in a horsebox to the swimming centre. Swimming commenced immediately and the duration of exercise was built up as rapidly as possible until the horse was swimming for about 10–12 minutes daily. After three weeks the horse's swimming was gradually combined with light ridden exercise until a normal routine was achieved. This return to normal training was achieved far more quickly than if the horse had been kept in his box. The horse went on to win more point-to-point races.

For back problems

Swimming is also a good form of exercise for horses with some types of back trouble. However, the advice of a good osteopath or chiropractor should always be sought before swimming, so as not to aggravate any particular case for which it might not be advisable. Swimming often brings unnoticed back problems to light, for horses tend to show that they are experiencing discomfort in their backs more easily in the pool than on ridden exercise. A horse swimming naturally is horizontal in the water; a horse that experiences discomfort will drop the hindquarters – a clear sign that there is something not quite right.

For psychological effects

A horse that is rested because of an injury can become very anxious if stabled for long periods without exercise. Even if horses are walked out, they will still not be able to burn off built-up energy, especially if previously quite fit, and may become excitable. Swimming can help to reduce the effects of confinement in such cases, as it will provide enough exertion to burn off any excess energy, thus keeping the horse more relaxed and in a calmer frame of mind. Once put back into normal exercise, the horse will be in far less danger of jumping about excitely and possibly damaging the injury again.

Some competition horses may simply tire of their

workload and routine and become uncooperative. Swimming, alternated with other forms of exercise, can offer something different which often freshens horses up, giving them a new outlook on their work.

Occasionally a horse may have great psychological problems. Usually, such a horse does not want anything to do with a normal training programme and makes life difficult for everybody. This is often due to a lack of self-confidence as a result of lack of trust in humans, who may have let the horse down in the past in some way. When swimming is brought into the programme for such horses, the results are often quite dramatic. Although they may try to refuse to swim at first, once in the pool they have to swim, or they will sink. They soon realize that this is an activity that they can do on their own and one which, to a certain extent, they are in control of. Self-confidence is increased and the horse once more becomes interested in life. Work can then begin on rebuilding trust.

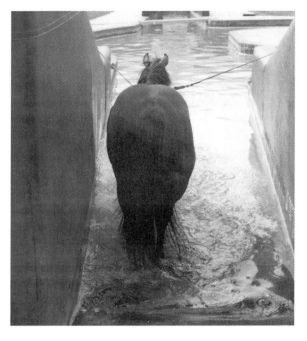

Swimming can give a horse a fresh outlook.

CASE HISTORY

FLINT: 12.2 hh, dapple grey show pony, 14 years old. This pony pricked his foot 12 days before a prestigious showing event. The foot became infected and the pony was very lame. The attending veterinary surgeon was able to pare the hoof to release the pus, enabling the condition to heal. However, as the pony felt pain each time he put his foot to the floor he was unable to be ridden. Knowing that the pony would be far too frisky at the show if he was not worked sufficiently prior to the event, the owner decided to swim him.

The pony was swum for nine days and ridden and swum for the last two days. The pony attended the event and qualified for the championships. The owner was quick to praise the value of swimming and insisted that the water also helped to put that 'little something extra' into the pony's coat, giving an overall picture of health and vitality.

Swimming: the only form of exercise where horses take in deep breaths of oxygen, shut off their nostrils for a few seconds, then forcibly blow it out again.

FITNESS TRAINING

Swimming not only helps injured horses but also provides alternative exercise for sound horses in dry, 'rock-hard' summer conditions, when normal outdoor exercise might jar their legs. It is also suitable for overweight horses whose weight might damage their limbs were they exercised normally. Additionally, it can assist the training programmes of horses with some conformation defect, who nevertheless show great potential in one sphere or another, where normal exercise would put strain on the fault. Such exercise can actually replace the work done on the ground and in such circumstances can prevent injury. It also helps to relax and unwind horses who tend to become nervous and anxious when they are very fit.

Swimming is the only form of exercise in which horses take in deep breaths of oxygen, shut off their nostrils for a few seconds and then forcibly blow it out, which can greatly improve cardiovascular fitness. However, horses fit enough to sustain a canter for a period of time cannot be expected to exchange normal work for the equivalent hydroexercise. They need a course of sessions to build up to an equivalent fitness level and to be maintained at that level. A direct comparison cannot be made between the level of fitness of a regularly exercised horse and one who is undergoing hydroexercise, for some horses are very energetic swimmers while others are lazy. Each horse does need to be taken as an individual.

At some point, though, a level is reached where a horse achieves maximum hydro-fitness. This is on average between eight to ten circuits of a pool that is 60 metres (yd) around. A session of ten circuits would take about four or five minutes to complete, in which the horse would swim roughly 600 m (yd).

This would be the equivalent of a six or seven furlong canter.

A horse can be got half fit by doing nothing but swimming, but it is a means to an end. Once the horse is right and the conditions are suitable, the normal training pattern should be resumed to achieve peak fitness.

Maintenance swimming

Swimming will also maintain a horse at peak fitness for a period of 10–12 days, which could mean the difference between competing in an important event or not. For example, St Leger winner Michelozzo pricked his foot just before the race but a few days of hydroexercise allowed him to be kept fully fit without putting any pressure on the injured foot. Henry Cecil, trainer of Michelozzo, was quoted in the *Racing Post* as saying: 'Without the pool it would have been impossible to get him to the race at all.'

Measuring the effects

While the benefits of a horse's swimming sessions become clear, it does help if there is some proof of the improved fitness as the sessions progress. This can be achieved with similar methods to those employed in interval training. Heart-rate values are a good indication of whether the horse is coping with the effort of swimming a certain distance, and readings can be taken before and after swimming (and possibly while swimming) at each session. The recovery rates are then measured after each swim and so a record of the fitness levels of the horse can be drawn up. It should show a steady improvement in fitness as time goes by.

If horses are swum for too long they become fatigued and the heart rate will rise above that recorded under normal swimming exertion. The sessions will be of no benefit and may even be harmful.

Introducing Horses to Swimming

Getting horses used to swimming is like any other equestrian activity: the golden rule of 'little and often' applies. They learn to accept that there is nothing to fear and soon come to enjoy their sessions.

As with introducing green horses to strange objects or jumps, they should be allowed to have a good look and a sniff when they first encounter the water. If they are still a little reluctant to venture in after they have had time to settle, then a rein is used from behind the quarters to urge them quietly forward – similar to when boxing horses who just need a little reassurance.

Very little equipment is needed to swim horses safely. A nylon headcollar is used with two reins (one attached at either side); one rein goes over the bridge of the nose on the near side. At some pools

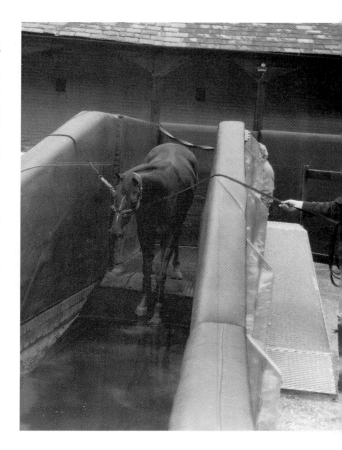

When a horse first encounters the water he should be allowed to have a good look.

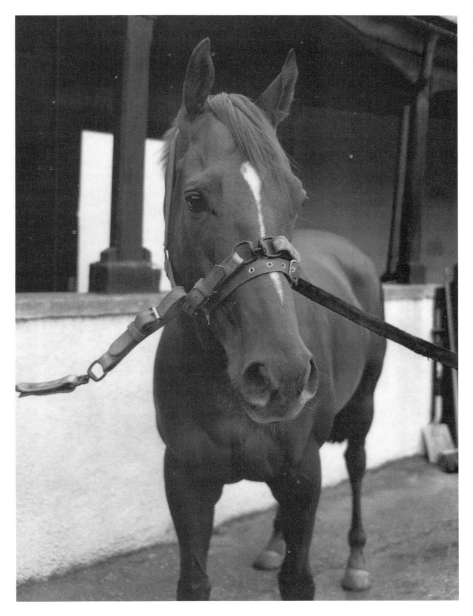

For swimming a nylon headcollar is used with two reins, one attached on each side.

horses are swum with only one rein and one handler, but for safety it is preferable to have two handlers in attendance. For the first few sessions, boots are put on the front legs because, although horses do not actually strike into themselves with their normal swimming motion, there is a possibility that they might knock themselves until they realize that they have to walk up and down a ramp.

As the benefits of hydroexercise and hydrotherapy become more widely known and accepted, this alternative activity will immensely improve all spheres of equestrianism. The whole process of swimming and possibly treadmill exercise, combined with the relaxing effect of a sand roll and the solarium (see page 44) is certainly an experience which any hard-worked horse deserves.

THE COST OF SWIMMING

Very few people have the money or space to install a purpose-built swimming pool, nor would it be worth the outlay unless there is a whole string of competition horses. What, then, are the options and how much would it cost? As swimming for horses is becoming increasingly popular, more trainers are installing pools. There are also equine therapy centres which have their own pools. These are expensive to maintain and many yards will swim your horse for you at a set fee to help fund the running costs. It may surprise you to learn that you can swim a horse for less than the cost of a single private lesson by a good instructor. However, it does become costly if your horse needs swimming on a regular basis. Whether the cost is worth it will depend on how valuable the benefits will be to you. For instance, if your horse bruises his sole a couple of weeks before a major event, you are likely to take the option of swimming him to maintain his fitness so that you can still compete – the chance to compete will outweigh the cost of swimming. On the other hand, if a child's pony bruises his sole, you probably would not give swimming a second thought.

FACILITIES

Centres that install pools often install other facilities such as scrape-down areas, sand rolls, infra-red solarium units and possibly a treadmill. Some centres also have a covered ride, which may be used as a collecting ring when dealing with racehorses in the summer months, as some pools have been known to swim as many as 60–70 horses per day at the height of the season. Some of those that initially catered mainly for the racing world now swim many different types of horse, from show-hunter ponies to three-day eventers.

After swimming, the horse is scraped down using an ordinary sweat scraper in a designated area. The sand rolls then provide an excellent 'letting-down' area where the horse can roll away the itchiness of being wet. Most horses seem to really like getting into the sand rolls: they benefit from a pleasurable experience after the exertion of swimming.

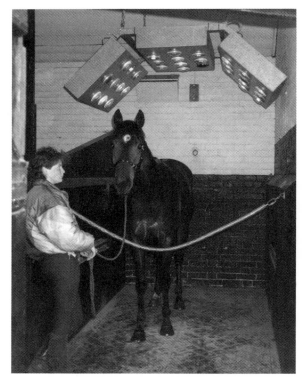

Drying off and relaxing in the infrared solarium.

After the sand roll, horses are usually put under the infra-red solarium to help them dry off and relax. The sand dries quickly under the heat (which can be regulated) and it is then easily brushed off.

Where a centre has all these facilities, they are all usually included within the standard swimming fee. The fee also includes the cost of professional handling from the minute the horse is ready to go into the pool to the minute he steps out. The first session is often given as a free trial, which allows the horse to become accustomed to a new activity and enables an assessment to be made of what sessions the horse might require. Although horses swim naturally, they do take a few sessions to obtain a relaxed action. Therefore the horse is initially just walked in, swum up the straight for about 25 metres (yd) and then taken out.

Combined swim-and-treadmill sessions can be arranged for any horse which it is thought will benefit, whether for therapy or exercise.

Pool designs

The design of equine swimming pools often gives cause for debate. They vary from a simple straight 'in-and-out' type to the oval-shaped pool, or one which combines a straight and round pool. The proprietor of a straight pool will be quick to extol its virtues, while those who have round pools will be just as quick to commend their design. There is no proof than one is better than the other and the horse owner would be better served by ensuring the horse is swum by an experienced handler rather than worrying about the shape of the pool. To a large extent the horse owner must trust the knowledge and experience of the handlers. Obviously too small a round pool will mean that the horse is swimming 'bent', while too short a straight pool will serve little purpose as the horse is forever getting in and out.

Perhaps the ideal incorporates a straight swim with a round pool. Horses can use the straight swim while they are being introduced to the activity. When they have become used to it they will then swim circuits of the pool, increasing the number of circuits as desired.

The best pools have every conceivable safety feature including in-and-out non-slip, padded ramps so that a quick exit can be made if required. One example (the BBA's Hastings Centre at Newmarket in the UK) is 3 metres (11 feet) deep and 60 metres (yd) around: on average a horse can complete two circuits per minute. It also has electric ram bridges across the entry and exit chutes for the handlers to walk across once the horse is swimming.

Pools are treated with chlorine and dry acid – the same as any human swimming pool – and most modern pools have a computerized filtration and purification plant to keep the chemicals at the correct levels. This prevents the risk of any disease transmission from whatever source, so that open wounds, for example, do not affect the hygiene of pools. When horses worth considerable sums of money are involved, safety and hygiene must be maintained to the highest possible standard.

Handlers – a special equestrian skill

It is essential that only fully experienced people actually swim the horses, as it is a tricky, potentially dangerous job made to look easy by the professionals. Because swimming should be as pleasurable an activity as possible for horses, handlers have to recognize when the horses have had enough and not let them get fatigued. It takes a trained eye to notice

Only fully experienced people should actually swim horses.

the signs. Horses also use some muscles when swimming which they would not in regular exercise and so a controlled build-up is essential.

Only the most experienced equine swimming handlers, who all see safety as of paramount importance, should be employed in hydroexercise centres. There should be a head swimmer with an enormous amount of experience both in the swimming of horses and in the knowledge of why and when to swim.

Teaching a horse to swim properly is very important. Horses that are simply allowed to plunge in may frighten themselves so much that they will always be tense when swimming in the future. Tense horses cannot use their muscles properly and the activity becomes non-productive. The aim when swimming horses is to make sure they enjoy what they are doing.

Specialist back-up

Most centres do not have a resident veterinary surgeon as the majority of clients have sought the advice of their own vet in advance. However, horses for whom swimming sessions are purely an alternative form of exercise do not need veterinary referral. An experienced swimming handler should be able to advise whether swimming would be suitable for a particular horse and on a possible fitness programme, either through swimming only or through swimming combined with treadmill exercise.

Many centres interact with animal therapists (if there is not a resident one) who will often come to treat horses for individual owners after their exercise in the pool.

Jacuzzis

Some swimming pools may also incorporate jacuzzi jets to provide a water massage as the horse swims. Where a water treadmill or water walk incorporates jacuzzi jets, these can often be regulated to massage certain areas – the tendons or shoulders, for example. In some cases this is accomplished by turning on a certain set of jets, while in others the jets themselves are adjustable. The water temperature can be regulated according to the condition being treated.

WATER WALKS

Water walks can be specially constructed or natural. A water walk is simply a place where a horse can be walked around in a depth of water. Purpose-built ones are more convenient as the temperature and depth can often be regulated and handlers can walk the horses alongside. Taking your horse down to your local stream may be your only option, and you may have to don waterproof footwear and get in too! However, the benefits are still valuable. Walking through water requires more effort for the horse (try walking in a swimming pool yourself and you will get the idea). This helps to strengthen the limbs and the water will also have a cushioning and soothing effect which will reduce concussion on the legs.

HOSE BOOTS

These range from a boot which looks and is fitted like a tendon boot, but to which a hose can be attached, to a fully moulded boot into which the horse's whole foot is placed. The tendon-like boot provides a cooling effect to help in cases of sprained tendons and the like, while moulded boots can have water put into them which is cold or hot, according to the therapeutic action required – keeping swelling down, for instance. Many such boots also have jacuzzi jets which help to massage and stimulate the lower legs and aid circulation.

HOSING

Cold-hosing is a good old-fashioned remedy which is often overlooked. It can aid many conditions and can be done by the owner. The important point to bear in mind when hosing is that pressure should be used. While a continuous trickle down the leg may cool an injured part, pressure will have a far greater effect. Pressure-hosing can help to stimulate circulation, thus speeding the healing process. It can also help to reduce proud flesh build-up on wounds.

Pressure should be used when cold-hosing as this stimulates circulation.

5 PHYSIOTHERAPY

Physiotherapy is simply the treatment of injury by mechanical or physical methods. Such methods range from the conventional use of cold hosing to the use of lasers and magnetic field treatments. Through a combination of hands-on care and recent technology, there has been a dramatic improvement in the possibilities for treatment of injuries by physiotherapy. Much of the work that is now covered by physiotherapists would have been considered incurable a decade ago.

Today, more horses are required to perform at high levels in various fields, including the show ring, where horses need to have a completely unblemished appearance. Any remaining scar tissue or a slight unevenness of gait can result in the horse being knocked down the line, which is extremely frustrating if the horse is otherwise a genuine animal. In the light of recent developments in physiotherapy, these horses need no longer be discarded to the hunting field or riding school. Through a combination of conventional therapy and physiotherapy many of these animals can now return to their previous form without any remaining blemish whatsoever.

While physiotherapy can work wonders in such 'cosmetic' cases, it has a far wider spectrum of application and is highly versatile in its approach. It can be just as beneficial in offering the geriatric horse a better quality of life, as in its ability to aid bone healing.

CAUSES OF INJURY

There are many causes of injury for which physiotherapy might be indicated. Those most commonly encountered include:
- Muscle, ligament and tendon strains due to lack of fitness.
- Forcing the horse into an outline by strapping down with tack, or by poor technique when training, producing back and neck trouble.
- Faulty conformation, which puts strain on muscles and joints through poor action.
- Ill-fitting tack or incompetent rider.
- Riding the horse in deep going, such as heavy mud, or deep sand schools, resulting in tendon pulls.
- Riding the horse on hard going, resulting in concussion.
- Accidental damage; a fall in the field or becoming cast in the stable for example.
- Tooth problems.
- Poor shoeing.

THE THERAPEUTIC PROCESS

Physiotherapy aims to produce the best environment in which the natural healing process can take place. Treating soon after injury will provide optimum results but old injuries can also be helped. The natural healing process goes through a pattern of changes:
- Blood supply is increased to the injured area.
- Increased fluid, produced as a result of the damage, causes swelling.
- Damaged nerve endings produce pain.
- A swelling of clotted blood in the tissues (haematoma) is caused by the creation of toxins from the damaged cells and the increased blood supply.
- Proliferation occurs (usually about a week after injury). New blood vessels, cells and collagen fibres grow into the haematoma creating scar tissue.
- Remodelling takes place (although this will takes months rather than weeks). The body will try to rebuild the injury back to its original condition.

TABLE 2: SUMMARY OF COMMON AVAILABLE TREATMENTS

LASER

Surface wounds
maintain stitches
wire cuts
scar tissue
stake wounds
post-operative
mud fever

Fetlock
direct trauma
joint jarring (sesamoids)
windgalls
abrasions

Hoof
bruised soles
quarter cracks
corns
penetrating injury
laminitis
heel bug
over reach

Leg
tendon strains
ligament strains
splint

Stifle
patella ligament strain

Knee
direct trauma
broken knee
post-operative

Hock
direct trauma
capped hock (acute)
curbs
tarsal ligament strain

Shoulder & withers
deltoid strain
withers spondylosis
girth galls

Back
muscle spasm
muscle damage
saddle abrasion
pressure lumps

ULTRASOUND

Torn muscles
Bursitis
Inflamed joints
Trauma knee
Windgalls
Scar tissue
Adhesion in tissue
Strained tendons
Strained muscles
Haematomas

ELECTROTHERAPY

Nerve-damaged muscles
Maintains muscle
  movement
Builds atrophied muscle

FARADISM

Breakdown of muscle
  spasms
Improves lymphatic
  drainage
Maintains muscle
  movement
Prevents adhesion after
  injury
Tonification of muscles

OTHER MACHINES

Magnetic foil pads
Hand friction units

METHODS OF TREATMENT

There are various methods available to the animal therapist. Those most widely used include:

- Laser
- Magnetic field
- Ultrasound
- Massage
- Faradism
- Trophic electrical stimulation
- Hot and cold therapy
- Passive movements
- Extensive exercise programmes.

As with any injury or illness there will always be the exception – one that will not respond to the given treatment, or one that is contraindicated for a specific form of therapy. Indeed, it is for this reason that therapy should only be applied by someone with sufficient knowledge to take everything into consideration and provide a therapy programme accordingly. No horse owner should expect an immediate miracle cure: therapy is a process, not an event.

The equipment

Modern developments have led to the introduction of a variety of incredibly expensive pieces of gadgetry which claim to be able to perform miracles. These machines are often referred to as 'idiot-proof', enticing horse owners into a false sense of security, thinking they can do no harm. These machines are often a waste of money: if they can do no harm, they are unlikely to do any good either. However, various developments have revolutionized animal care.

LASER

Laser therapy is referred to as LLLT (low reactive level laser therapy). The laser light, emitted from either a cluster or a single probe, penetrates the injured area and stimulates the natural healing process within the damaged tissues. When the energy of the beam of light travels into tissues, it stimulates the metabolism and production of collagen (which is the main protein of skin, bone, cartilage, connective tissue and tendon) and thus stimulates the rate of repair and remodelling.

CASE HISTORY

PADDY: 16.2 hh, dark bay filly, show horse. This filly had an off-fore wound which had cut through the common digital extensor tendon. She was 'hopping' lame and extremely anxious. The veterinary surgeon referred her to an animal therapist for treatment.

The filly received 60 laser treatments over a period of six weeks, with on average ten treatments a week. The wound healed remarkably well and although there is still slight thickening at the site of the injury the horse is perfectly sound. She is competing in the show ring, with moderate success, although she has never been put down the line due to her old injury.

While laser is not a universal panacea, there are various conditions that may be indicated for its use (Tables 2 and 3). Very often laser will form only part of a treatment which may also include electro-therapy, ice, mobilization, topical application dressings and the like.

Lasers have an *antibacterial effect*, which makes them particularly suitable for treating *open wounds*, but their use alone in severe wound therapy is not sufficient; in fact, without the benefit of antibiotics laser therapy can be detrimental, especially in the presence of infection. For best results, therefore, laser therapy should be used in conjunction with conventional therapy – antibiotics and stitches

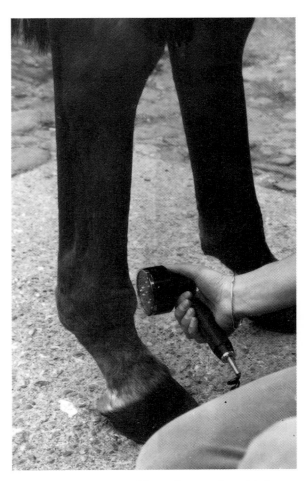

The light energy discharged from a laser can be emitted from a cluster . . .

(where applicable), for example – or in conjunction with homoeopathy.

In treatment of *sports injuries*, laser therapy offers fast and safe rehabilitation and a shortened recovery time. It should be used as soon as possible after injury – ideally within minutes or hours, rather than days, as much quicker results will be achieved. Also, if treatment is started within 24 hours, 'proud flesh' does not usually occur and secondary infection is controlled. Wounds often heal without scarring and have normal hair growth. As with all aspects of horse management, best results are achieved by 'little and often' treatments – for example twice daily, or once in every four hours.

or from a single probe.

TABLE 3: USE OF LASER THERAPY

Main roles
Treatment of open wounds
Giving pain relief
Resolving inflammation
Increasing the speed, quality and tensile strength of tissue repair
Stimulating the immune system
Resolving infection
Improving the function of damaged neurological tissue

Clinical applications
Acute (fresh) injuries
Chronic scar tissue (old injuries)
Open wounds
Haematomas
Hoof conditions
Bruised soles, corns, cracking, soft hooves
Mud fever (boosts the immune system)
Reduction of swelling (acute injuries)
Tendon, muscle and ligament injuries
Arthritis (maintenance programme)
Stiff and tense muscles
Circulation stimulation
Sore shins
Tonification and acupuncture

Contraindications
Laser therapy should not be used:
- in conjunction with steroids or any form of cortisone, as laser produces the same effect by stimulating natural cortisone
- for infected wounds
- where retina contact is likely

Magnetic Field Therapy (MFT)

The theory behind magnetic field therapy is that normal cells have a uniform arrangement of positively and negatively charged particles which are altered when the cell is damaged. This alteration restricts the flow of fluid, which results in swelling and thus pain. Magnetic field therapy aims to realign the charged particles, enabling a free flow of fluid to be resumed.

MFT reduces healing time by increasing blood circulation and the rate at which calcium is released (the effects of the treatment are cumulative) and so it is often indicated for *fractures*. It can be used safely in the presence of casts, nails, screws and plates without loss of efficiency.

MFT is one of the most effective methods of relieving *muscular spasms*. It is also beneficial in offering *geriatric horses* a better quality of life in their remaining years: it is thought that its rejuvenating effects occur because MFT increases circulation and the level and utilization of oxygen in the system. It also offers mild *pain relief*.

Pulsed magnetic field (PMF)

The PMF has three parameters:
- Time (the treatment time)
- Intensity (the strength of the magnetic field), which determines the depth of penetration
- Frequency (the pulses per second), which determines the biological effects.

When used at frequencies between 4 and 6 Hz, PMF treatment reduces blood flow. When used at over 10 Hz, it produces vasodilation and thus improved oxygenation to assist in healing. At more than 25 Hz it stimulates the release of calcium within the bone. Thus the different frequencies are used to treat different conditions (see Table 4).

Magnavet therapy shapes

Magnavet therapy shapes apply a magnetic force to the skin and tissues at the point of application: they produce an alternating field and retain their magnetism. They are available to fit specific areas such as the tendon, shin, fetlock, knee, coronet, hock and back, and the shapes can be cut to size over splints

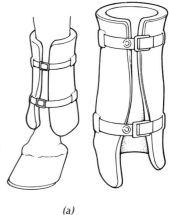

Magnavet therapy shapes: (a) tendon; (b) tendon and shin; (c) knee; (d) fetlock.

(a)

Table 4: Use of PMF
Main roles
Reduce oedema
Fractures
Tendon injuries
Back problems, including deep back injuries
Splints
Paralysis
Arthritis
At 4–6 Hz
• To help reduce oedema and offer pain relief during acute inflammatory stages
• To stop breakdown of stitches when a bruised area has also been cut
At more than 25 Hz
• To aid the healing of fractures
• To stimulate a chronic (old) injury into an acute (recent) injury to assist in treatment
Contraindications
PMF should not be used on:
• infected wounds
• pregnant animals
• over joints on young animals (it may stimulate bone growth)

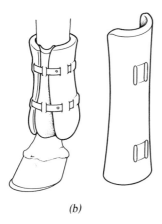

(b)

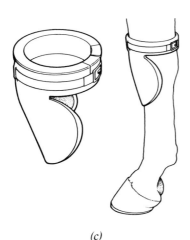

(c)

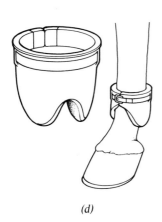

(d)

or other protrusions. They are used in the treatment of a wide range of ailments involving tissue, muscle, tendon or ligament damage.

ULTRASOUND

Ultrasound (Table 5) is based on pressure waves of specific wavelength, frequency and velocity, travelling through a medium such as water. A quartz or barium titanate crystal is fused to the metal plate of a transducer or treatment head. When the crystal is bombarded with high frequency current, movement occurs within it and is transmitted to the metal front plate, producing ultrasonic waves.

TABLE 5: USE OF ULTRASOUND
Benefits Thermal effects Vibrations for micromassage Deep penetration of the tissue Chronic injuries become more acute Safe treatment for horses on anti-inflammatory drugs **Applications** Relaxation of muscle spasms (thermal effects) Increase of blood supply to a repairing area in treatment of: • tendon trouble • laminitis • back complaints Breaking down of scar tissue and adhesions Prevention of some of scar tissue formation in early stages Treatment of haematomas (ultrasound travels through fluids) **Contraindications** Ultrasound should not be used on: • suspected fractures • inflamed injuries

Ultrasound is a powerful tool and can be dangerous in inexperienced hands. The vibrations could actually cause bone breakage, especially if a fracture is already suspected. Misapplication of ultrasound could also result in joint fluid being overheated, or the bone membrane (periosteum) being scorched, as the thermal effects can intensify around bone, causing severe pain. The thermal effects also preclude the use of ultrasound on acutely inflamed injuries, though it can be used on a very low setting in the early treatment of tendon injuries to reduce the swelling.

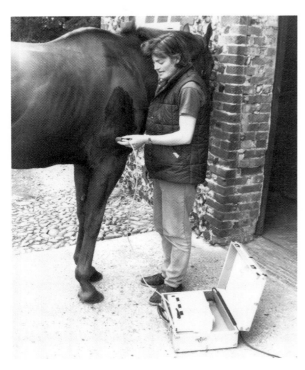

Ultrasound is a powerful tool which can be dangerous in inexperienced hands.

A small hand-held massager being used on the lower legs to improve venous return.

MASSAGE MACHINES

Hand massage techniques are described in detail in Chapter 6. There is a wide variety of machine massagers, ranging from small hand-held units to the large Niagara massager. The therapist moves the massager in a linear direction similar to that of the fibres, using firm but even pressure. Greater pressure is used over the muscle bulk than over bony prominences. The effect of these machines is that of vibration, of varying depth. The small hand-held units can be used on the lower legs to improve venous return. The large Niagara massagers (Equissage) can be strapped on to the horse for use but, as with other machinery, it is important to accustom the horse to the feel and sound first.

Machine massagers are very beneficial before and after exercise as a warm-up and to prevent the horse from cooling down too quickly, especially after particularly strenuous exercise. They can also be used to aid soft tissue repair, to support scarring, bruises, windgalls, thoroughpins (swellings level with the hock) and filled joints.

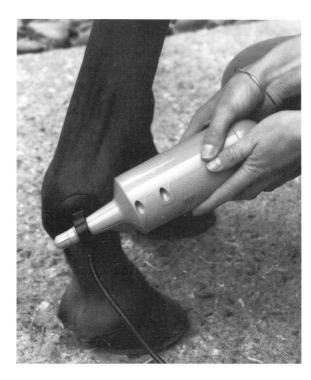

The **equissage** is a custom-built massage pad designed for the larger areas of shoulder, back, loins or haunches. It is designed to mould itself to the individual contours of a horse and can be easily secured by means of straps which are built into D-rings, similar to those on a saddle. It promotes repair by opening the lymph ducts throughout the horse, thus removing toxins that are creating inflammation. It is intended for use after muscular injury, after strenuous exercise, after long journeys, during enforced idleness, to maintain muscle tone, to stimulate circulation, to supple up and to improve performance.

Massaging local areas with a hand-held ice cube is especially good in acute, very recent injuries with inflammation.

How the Equissage is applied to (a) the shoulders; (b) the back; (c) the loins; (d) the croup and thighs and (e) to give an overall massage.

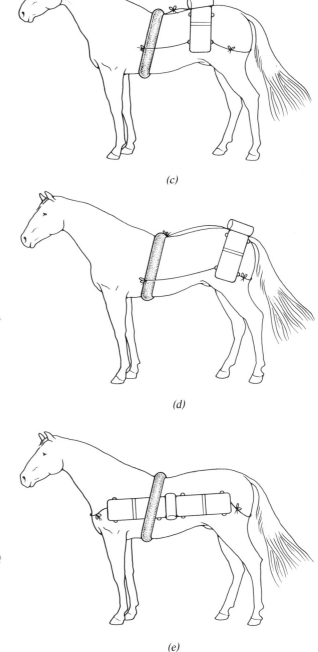

(c)

(a)

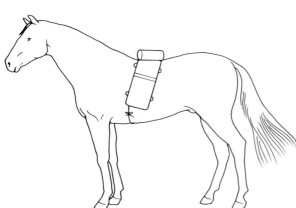

(b)

(d)

(e)

FARADISM

This is a rhythmic stimulation of the muscles by emitting a Faradic electric current into the motor nerve of the muscle. The aim is to mimic the natural rhythmic contractions of muscles. The body cannot move without muscle activity and movement influences every bodily system. It is therefore of prime importance to maintain muscle capability after injury and this can be achieved by Faradism. It can be both diagnostic and therapeutic, and although it has to some extent been superseded by trophic electrical stimulation it is still a valuable method. The Electrovet model also has galvanic stimulation, which is used extensively on tendon injury and gives the equivalent of weightless exercise. The horse is kept on this therapy for up to and sometimes in excess of one hour in the stable to prepare tendon injury for the start of exercise. These machines are also used on sore shins.

Faradic machines aim to mimic the natural rhythmic contractions of muscles.

CASE HISTORY

SAMPSON: 16.3 hh, grey gelding, 12-year-old endurance horse. The owner of this horse noticed that he was not moving evenly when on the right diagonal. The veterinary surgeon called upon the assistance of an equine physiotherapist to offer an opinion on probable cause.

On examination, muscular contraction of the right hindquarter revealed areas of poor muscle response. Non-elasticity of the muscles therefore caused uneven gait on the right diagonal.

The horse received three faradic treatments within the first week and he responded well. A further six faradic treatments were given within the following two weeks and the horse also underwent swimming exercise combined with intensive schooling. The horse responded well to treatment and is now using the right hind as normal.

*A neuromuscular stimulator
securely applied.*

NEUROMUSCULAR STIMULATOR

By applying the correct neuromuscular stimulator
to a motornerve, the muscle fibre will be activated
leading to actual structural alterations of the fibre.
As the motor neurone controls the fibre, certain
patterns of stimulation produce the enzymes which
influence active and healthy working muscles. Uses
include:

- Muscle re-education
- Prevention or retardation or muscle atrophy
- Increase local blood circulation
- Maintain muscle motion.

H-WAVE

The H-Wave is a relatively new machine for the treatment of tissue damage and pain. Its signal can be applied in two ways: by using low frequency or high frequency impulses. The low frequency therapy mode triggers muscle contractions which result in an increase in the flow of oxygenated blood through the site of an injury, stimulating lymphatic drainage. As a result oedema and swelling are reduced. High frequency impulses afford a deep local anaesthesia, without muscle stimulation. This is very beneficial when treating acutely painful conditions as the H-Wave can be applied to anaesthetize the damaged area before proceeding with low frequency therapy treatment. Unfortunately, the H-Wave varies enormously in the anaesthesia effect from animal to animal and so care must be taken.

CASE HISTORY

BILL: 15.3 hh, chestnut gelding, riding club horse. This horse was referred for physiotherapy from a veterinary surgeon. A thickening of the muscle over the main trochanter showed some non-elasticity and there were signs of atrophied muscle above this region in the hindquarters. Sideways flexion of the neck was also restricted. Palpation of the lumbar region of the longissimus dorsi muscles and examination with the muscle stimulator revealed great pain and hypertension in the lumbar region of the back.

A two-week course of electrotherapy using mainly the H-Wave machine was carried out, together with laser treatment in the early stages to reduce pain.

On re-examination, when palpating the lumbar region, the muscles appeared softer and pain free. With a gradual work programme, the horse's hindquarters were built up and became stronger. Daily exercises with the neck relieved the stiffness. An increase in the length of stride at trot was observed and lateral flexion was improved.

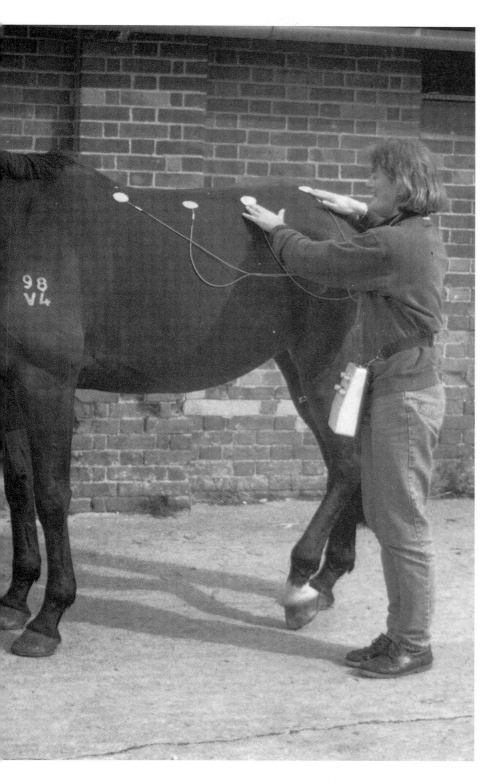

The H-Wave, a relatively new machine used in the treatment of tissue damage and pain.

TROPHIC ELECTRICAL STIMULATION

Trophic electrical stimulation is tolerated well by horses. It has many benefits in the treatment of muscle conditions. It can:

- maintain the muscle's metabolism;
- improve venous return;
- aid lymphatic drainage;
- help to prevent massive muscle atrophy;
- reduce scar tissue;
- re-educate weakened muscle.

TENS (TRANSCUTANEOUS ELECTRICAL NERVE STIMULATORS

TENS machines are more widely known in the veterinary field as Dr Pulse units. They are used to overpower pain. The pain signals from an injured site are blocked by a pulsed signal emitted through electrodes placed on the skin. These need to be used sensibly as pain is a warning which should not be ignored. Ultimately what is causing the pain needs to be established.

TENS machines are more widely known in the veterinary field as Dr Pulse units.

HOT AND COLD THERAPY

Cold therapy takes many forms: cold hosing, tubbing, ice packs, specially designed cold boots and Bonner bandages or even standing in a running stream, for example – in fact anything that safely cools the area being treated. The aim is to increase circulation in the affected area and as a result reduce swelling. The application of a cooling medium results in the constriction and dilation of blood vessels, producing a pumping action which, as desired, increases the circulation. When applying ice, it is important not to put it directly on to the skin as this can cause ice burns.

Heat therapy also takes many forms, from applying hot poultices or tubbing in hot water, to using infra-red lamps. Heat therapy is mostly used to help relax muscles, dilate blood vessels and soothe pain. As with any therapy, heat needs to be used sensibly to avoid scorching. If hot water-bottles or specialized heat packs are used, they should be wrapped in a towel.

Initially, many conditions will benefit from just applying cold therapy to prevent further inflammation and swelling of the affected area, but as treatment commences it is more beneficial to use alternating hot and cold treatments, as this increases the circulation and aids in the dispersion of existing swelling. The use of cold therapy after laser or MFT will have the same effect.

PASSIVE MOVEMENT

This is used to help maintain mobility of a joint during injury. The joint is supported above and below and is then gently moved through its full range of movement.

It is often beneficial to give massage and/or heat therapy before passive movement as this will get the blood flow going. With passive movement the circulation increases slightly and the muscles are all flexed and extended. However, there is no active muscle action as it is the therapist who is moving the joint, not the horse.

In addition to a decline in efficiency of the vital cardiovascular and respiratory systems, confinement in excess of about a week results in a loss of protein and enzymes from muscles, demineralization of bone and a deficiency in joint cartilage and synovia. Active exercise must therefore start as soon as possible, by implementing a rational exercise programme of ascending intensity over a period in order to restore tissue loss and functional strength. Active exercise entails voluntary muscle contraction by the horse and includes all types of exercise from walking to swimming and hydrotherapy.

When walking exercise commences after a period of confinement and box rest, it should begin on ground that has a little 'give' in it, such as a moist, grassy surface. This reduces the jarring or dynamic force on weakened limbs that occurs when limbs impact on hard ground, such as concrete or a road surface. However, soft, boggy ground is not good for tendon injuries as pulling feet out of deep going causes unnecessary strain. Once the horse has had a week or so of walking on a grassy surface he is best walked around the yard for another week, to provide a mild concussive force which will harden weaker areas, tightening up tendons before the horse is turned out in the field.

RE-EDUCATION OF MOVEMENT

During injury, horses may adapt their movement to avoid causing themselves any unnecessary pain; shuffling, moving stiffly and coming up short (shortening the stride) are good examples. Once the injury has healed, horses often retain the habit of the adapted movement and it can be difficult to persuade them to revert to their former paces. Rehabilitation or 're-education' is needed.

The horse needs to regain his faith in where to place his limbs confidently in relation to his body. He will often need reassuring that if he steps out correctly he will not receive pain any more. The only way the therapist can achieve this is to make the horse move in such a way that he will have to use the strides that once gave him pain. Working over trotting poles can often achieve this, which can be done in a circle, on a straight line or with the poles raised. Swimming and treadmill therapy are also used in re-educating movement.

Where horses are shut up all day they can develop anxiety problems which may result in a vice such as crib-biting.

MENTAL THERAPY

Where horses are shut up in a stable for much of the day they may develop anxiety problems. To alleviate their distress they should be placed out at grass as often as possible. They should also have a lot of attention and encouragement when around humans to keep them mentally stimulated. Make sure when they are stabled that they are comfortable and their needs are met – a happy patient means a faster recovery.

DIAGNOSTIC TECHNIQUES

All diagnosis must be carried out by a veterinarian alone, but it is possible that the physiotherapist may be able to aid the vet in diagnosis by using some of the equipment mentioned. This is especially true if the horse has a disguised condition. By stimulating the damaged area, the therapist will cause pain and the horse will flinch or try to move away. By slowly assessing the horse's reaction to each section of the suspected damaged area, the site of injury can be isolated. Some lasers also have pain finders. These are very useful when trying to establish how things are progressing, or even when trying to find out where the problem is.

Thermography

Thermography is a unique diagnostic aid in that there is no contact with the horse. It works by observing heat patterns, producing a complete thermal picture. This can be very beneficial in the early diagnosis of injury, stress or infection as the local temperature in the vicinity of the injury or infection rises. A thermograph will show this rise which will clearly indicate a problem, even if it cannot be detected by the human hand. However, every care must be taken as outside heat, such as sunlight through windows or cold draughts through doors, will alter the readings.

Any problem that results in a change in heat patterns can be monitored and these include, but are not limited to:

- Inflamed tendons
- Ligaments
- Laminitis
- Muscle strain
- Arthritis
- Knocks
- Circulation problems
- Fractures and navicular.

As thermographic scanning can ensure prompt detection of a wide range of problems, treatment costs and recovery times can be minimized.

WHO ARE EQUINE THERAPISTS?

Physiotherapy is only a valid form of treatment if it is applied by someone who understands how the various machines and appliances work. It is important to remember that technology alone can never entirely replace many of the traditional techniques that have been used on animals for centuries. A thorough knowledge of the anatomy and physiology of the horse, together with a true understanding of indications and contraindications, is required in order to administer treatment effectively. Furthermore, this knowledge and understanding alone is not sufficient to ensure successful therapy. Because it is not possible to ask where it hurts, diagnosing a precise problem is the hardest and most important part of any treatment. Therefore, before any therapy can commence a vet should always diagnose the nature of the ailment and decide whether physiotherapy should be administered. As vets are unlikely to have the necessary equipment or training to be able to use it properly, they will refer cases to trained animal physiotherapists.

There is no specific training for physiotherapists who wish to specialize in horses. At present entry is through qualifying as a chartered physiotherapist in the human field. A chartered therapist may then become a pupil with a veterinary practice or animal equine physiotherapist until two veterinary surgeons are prepared to certify that they have successfully transferred their skills from humans to animals.

The Association of Chartered Physiotherapists in Animal Therapy (ACPAT) holds a register of chartered animal therapists who are insured to treat animals. The main qualification for those specializing in horses is experience and many of today's equine physiotherapists have learned their skills through work experience with those already practising in the field.

Many equine therapists have an interest in horses generally and some are active horse people. This means that they have practical knowledge of horse management and riding, and can relate treatment to the work and stable routines of individual horses.

A body of practising animal therapists in the UK have set up a regulatory National Association of Animal Therapists. This group of therapists has been working exclusively on animals, most of them for 20 or more years; it is insured to work exclusively for the veterinary profession and its members work only on animals.

Physiotherapists who specialize in horses have had to earn every inch of the respect they have gained from the equestrian public. Only a few years ago, some vets were dubious about the skills of physiotherapists. Consequently it was a hard struggle for them to prove their worth in relation to equestrian sports therapy. Happily, most are now getting a really good response from numerous veterinary surgeons nationwide.

Horse owners have also been slow to recognize the many benefits of physiotherapy in treating horses' injuries and illnesses. To some extent this may be because owners were not given any information and so viewed physiotherapy as a mystery; in fact, many horse owners did not even know what physiotherapy actually was.

6 MASSAGE AND MANIPULATION

Massage is basically a rub-down of the muscles in order to relieve stress and to relax the horse, whereas manipulative techniques are used to alter the musculoskeletal system. Any horse owner can learn massage techniques which will be helpful to the horse in times of illness or injury, but musculo-skeletal manipulation must be reserved for the manipulative specialist who is usually a trained osteopath or chiropractor. Such manipulative ther-apies are nothing new: like many complementary treatments they can be traced back to ancient Chinese and Greek medicine.

CAUSES OF MUSCLE COMPLAINTS

Many horses can be ridden for several years without experiencing any kind of muscle or skeletal trouble, so why do some horses seem to suffer more than others? In the majority of cases, muscle disorders can be traced to a particular incident. They may become troublesome as a result of events such as a sharp blow or they may result from fatigue, over-stretching (where they may tear), cooling down too quickly (especially after overheating), incorrect posture or badly fitting shoes, a fever or disease, a structural or systematic imbalance or even poor nourishment.

High performance horses will suffer more than others as they are often required to give maximum physical effort which will stress their muscles con-siderably, especially if they have not been warmed up correctly beforehand. Because a muscle contracts in response to such stress, there can be uneven force on either an opposing muscle or a joint. This is

thought to be a contributory factor to many of the back complaints experienced by these horses.

BACK TROUBLE

Are back complaints simply the result of stresses and strains which are only to be expected in any athlete, equine or otherwise? The likelihood of back com-plaints in the horse is far greater than in humans and it is probably due to human demands that the horse suffers so. The horse is often subjected to unnatural activities, yet is assumed to be able to cope with the demands of such activities. The equine frame is physically unsuited to many competitive spheres and the horse's back is only one of the inherent design weaknesses.

How can back trouble be minimized? Firstly, investigate the most probable causes; secondly, armed with such information, consider how to alter our actions towards horses and our demands on their abilities.

It is fortunate that the horse is an amenable creature that seems quite happy, in most cases, to perform what is asked of him. Indeed, no caring rider would compete on a horse that did not seem to be enjoying himself. If a horse starts to lose form it is sensible to suspect that he is unhappy, for an unhappy horse never performs well. The first question to ask is: are the pressures of work too great? It is a question of distinguishing between hard work and overwork, because it is often over-work which causes the problems. Horses that have been properly prepared should be able to cope with hard work in an activity for which they have the necessary ability. It is when we ask that little bit too much too soon, or that difficult exercise just a few times too many that the horse's back and muscles start to take too much strain. While many horses will suffer from the odd twinge here and there, which cannot be prevented, the truth is that many horses' back complaints have their origins in human failure. It is only by creating a greater awareness amongst riders and horse owners that such back injuries can be reduced. Educating the rider and trainer as to what an individual horse is, and is not, able to accomplish without suffering overload to the supporting structure of the spine is most important when dealing with performance horses. The spine is a non-renewable resource.

SOURCES OF DAMAGE

Back trouble, whether skeletal or muscular, may be caused without any human interference – the horse may slip over when galloping around a slippery field, for instance – but such occurrences are rare. More common are back complaints caused by human interaction with the horse. Contributory factors may include:

- Pulling a foal incorrectly from its dam at birth
- Overworking the young horse
- Forcing a desired headcarriage by sheer brute strength or by using certain equipment
- Overworking the unfit horse
- Extensive schooling or lungeing on circles
- Falls when jumping
- Bad landings over fences
- An ill-fitting saddle.

It may be impossible to predict why a horse develops a back condition, especially if the horse has only recently been acquired and there is no knowledge of the previous history. Also, many problems manifest themselves elsewhere in the body. For example, fussy-mouthed horses are often found to have back problems which, once cured, generally leave the horse more tolerant in the mouth. It is also unwise to discount a physical problem in the back before labelling the horse as being 'cold-backed'. Similarly horses who will not stand still for mounting, or who

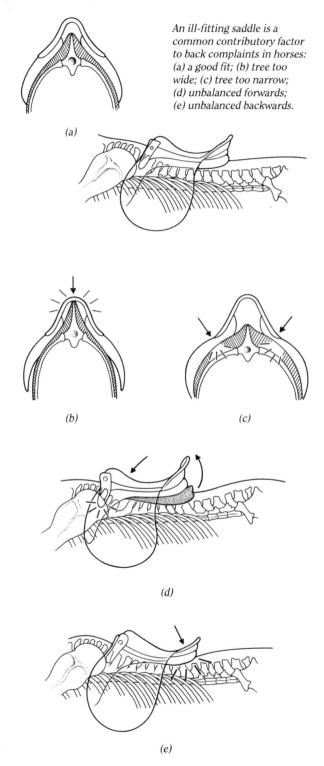

An ill-fitting saddle is a common contributory factor to back complaints in horses: (a) a good fit; (b) tree too wide; (c) tree too narrow; (d) unbalanced forwards; (e) unbalanced backwards.

(a)

(b)   (c)

(d)

(e)

'hump' their backs or even buck when first mounted, may have a back complaint.

All sorts of seemingly unrelated health or performance problems can also be traced to the horse's back due to painful pressures along the spinal column. Some classic symptoms of back conditions include:

- Unlevel movement
- Uneven strides
- Refusal to jump
- Uneasiness when trotting uphill or downhill
- Skewing over fences when jumping
- Uneasiness when saddling
- Continual bucking
- Inability to come off the forehand
- Inability to strike off on a certain canter lead
- Decreasing performance
- Reluctance to pick up a certain hoof
- Abnormal posture
- Grinding of the teeth.

Obviously not all problems emerge from displacements in the back but such symptoms are good indicators if a back problem is suspected.

ASYMMETRY

Before deciding to get specialized help for what appears to be a back problem, consider any natural causes. Just as most people are one-sided, so horses tend to favour one particular side. This can be noticed as a greater willingness to bend more on one rein than the other, usually to the left. The horse is naturally crooked, but there may be other contributory factors which exacerbate the problem and so lead to poor performance.

Poor conformation may affect symmetry in the horse, as may old injuries, an unbalanced rider or an ill-fitting saddle. The first symptom of asymmetry is a reluctance to turn on one rein because the horse actually finds it more difficult to do so. Other symptoms include constantly failing to perform a square halt, loss of impulsion during transitions, refusing or running out at fences when on the affected rein, lack of rhythm, swinging in of the quarters and tilting of the head.

Many riders sit crookedly and are a major cause of asymmetry in horses.

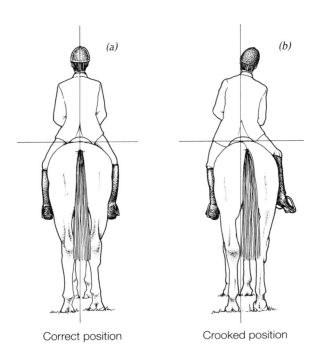

Correct position   Crooked position

How then do you find out why your horse is crooked and how can the problem be quickly rectified? Firstly eliminate yourself as a cause. Many riders sit crookedly and are totally unaware that they are doing so. This means the horse has to over compensate on one rein to achieve balance. Have someone video you while riding, showing you riding towards and away from the camera, as well as in circles and performing upward and downward transitions. Replay the tape and examine your position at all paces. You may be astonished to realize that you are sitting crooked, as your position will feel perfectly straight to you. When trying to correct your riding position you will have to make a really conscious effort to sit straight and at first you will feel as if you are leaning too far in the opposite direction. It is very beneficial to have an instructor observe you in the first few sessions to tell you when you are sitting straight. You will then know how 'straightness' feels and can work towards that feeling each time you ride on your own.

If you feel your riding posture is quite acceptable then you should lunge your horse to confirm that he still shows signs of one-sidedness. If he does, you will need to embark upon a re-schooling programme to 'straighten' him. However, before you do so also have his teeth, limbs and back checked by a vet, or else you may be trying to straighten some form of back trouble or injury, rather than a natural dominance of one side of your horse's body.

STRUCTURE OF THE HORSE'S BACK

Back problems can be very frustratingly hard to diagnose and it can take time for treatment to take effect. The back is a very complex piece of anatomy and it is helpful to have some knowledge of its structure.

The vertebral column is formed by a joined sequence of individual barrel-shaped vertebrae which are somewhat distant from the skin surface. The structures which can be felt under the skin surface are in fact dorsal spinous processes, beneath which lie the actual vertebrae. Each vertebra is flexibly connected with the one both behind and in front on several different levels, forming an extremely intricate joint. Muscle fibres, ligaments and dense connective tissue bind each vertebra to its immediate and distant neighbours in a complex structure. Therefore it is possible for the horse to move the spine in all directions, albeit by a very defined amount.

Back pain, other than that originating from soft tissue damage, is likely to come from main skeletal lesions. The pain is usually more evident when the

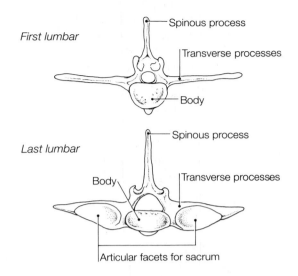

Above: The thoracic vertebrae.
Below: The dorsal spinous processes lie close to the skin surface under the saddle area.

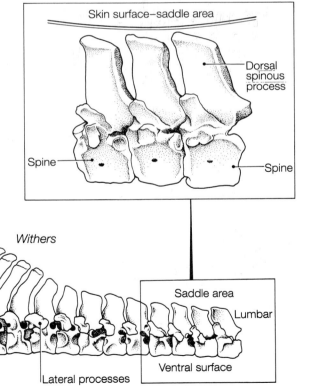

horse tries to flex the spine. This is due to an impingement of the dorsal spinal processes, which results in bone rubbing against bone, and thus leading to erosion.

BACK TREATMENT

Chiropractic and osteopathy are two forms of human treatment which have been adapted for horses. They are often described as two very different therapies, when in practice there is very little difference between the two groups as a whole: both use similar techniques and the therapies overlap considerably. They both treat similar conditions, and often their techniques vary more between practitioners than between the disciplines: one osteopath may be as different in technique to another osteopath as he or she is to a chiropractor. Both osteopaths and chiro-

practors treat the spine and nervous system for a range of problems.

The technical difference is that some osteopaths use leverage to a greater degree by twisting and exerting pressure at a place somewhat removed from the joint they are aiming to adjust, whereas chiropractors use a short, sharp 'thrust' on the joint itself.

The McTimoney technique of chiropractic

The chiropractic McTimoney technique is an innovative approach of analysis and treatment that is particularly suitable for animals. It is built on three basic principles: firstly, disease may be caused by disturbances of the nervous system; secondly, disturbances of the nervous system may be caused by

Chiropractors use a short, sharp thrust on the joint itself.

In Manu Vis Medendi

The McTimoney Chiropractic School logo.

derangements of the musculoskeletal structure; and thirdly, disturbances of the nervous system may cause or aggravate disease in various parts or functions of the body.

Because of the stresses that horses are called upon to bear, they are probably the single biggest group of animal chiropractic patients. The question of whether or not a horse's back can actually be 'put back in' is always cause for debate. Some say they are releasing muscle spasm, others that they are making adjustments that create the right environment for healing to take place. It is anatomically inaccurate to refer to a back being 'put back in', as vertebrae do not 'go out' in the first place. In truth, the only joints which are capable of moving during a spinal adjustment are the facet joints which link the vertebrae, and even if these should move the shift would be very slight.

What to expect from chiropractic treatment

Properly trained chiropractors have to undergo a rigorous course in manipulative theory and practice. They are competent and professional and are trained to manipulate the animal's musculoskeletal system with a high degree of skill.

The use of X-rays is widespread in the chiropractic profession, much more so than in the osteopathic

CASE HISTORY

HENRY: 16.2 hh dark bay gelding, 10-year-old, National Hunt chaser in full training. This horse was found in its box completely unable to move, sweating and trembling with pain and anxiety. The symptoms were diagnosed by the attending veterinary surgeon as probable nerve impingement in the neck, of unknown cause. The only way to confirm the diagnosis would be a myelogram (injection of a radio-opaque dye into the spinal canal, followed by X-ray). Since the horse was unable to put one foot in front of the other, this was out of the question.

Manipulation was performed with some trepidation on two vertebrae only, because of the extreme nature of symptoms. On a return visit two days later the horse was moving without much pain and eating and drinking normally. A full treatment was given at this time followed by two further treatments at weekly intervals. Three months later this horse came third in a try-out race at Sandown and continued his career without any repetition of the problem for a further three years, winning several races before a well earned retirement.

field. However, McTimoney chiropractors prefer to rely on a case history and their own palpatory skills to carry out an accurate assessment. Because it is illegal for McTimoney chiropractors to treat patients without a veterinary referral, the animals have usually had all the relevant veterinary diagnoses carried out, including X-rays, where necessary. Therefore, when chiropractors first attend a horse they will palpate the spine, looking for areas of dysfunction in the vertebral column. They will place a strong emphasis on the importance of re-balancing the entire skeletal structure, which means that they might manipulate the horse's neck or legs, when it is the back which appears to be the problem. The results of the assessment will indicate which part of the horse to manipulate.

The chiropractor will use more than one technique to treat the 'whole' body.

Horses can suffer from many back problems, from simple muscle strain to a full ligament tear. While chiropractors will use more than one technique to treat the 'whole' body, they will adjust vertebrae by using what is known as the 'toggle recoil' technique. This is an extremely light and fast movement of the hands on a specific part of the bone.

Results

The most desirable reaction to treatment is an immediate improvement in the horse, but be warned that the results of any individual treatment may not be seen until a few days or even weeks later, and more than one manipulative session may be needed. The horse's body is not a machine and so it is not quite as simple as changing a few plugs and putting things right. Chiropractic does deal with body mechanics, but the horse's body, unlike a machine, cannot be fixed immediately by changing an old, worn out part with a new one. Healing is a process, not an isolated event.

In general, most manipulators are called in because conventional treatment has failed to effect a cure; or because a horse has gone lame as a result of

CASE HISTORY

INTERNATIONAL GRADE A SHOW-JUMPER: 10-year-old grey gelding, 17 hh, which had competed regularly on the European show-jumping circuit. This horse had a history of back pain which had been controlled by intraspinous injection of analgesic – a technique much favoured in Europe because it controls the pain so that the horse can continue to be used, but the condition inevitably deteriorates.

In this case the horse's ability to jump was being seriously hindered by an increasingly stiffening back. This was relieved with manipulation over a number of weeks. The manipulation returned the horse to comfortable movement and increased the flexibility of his spine so that his jumping became more fluid.

a fall or other mechanical injury (although not if a fracture is suspected); or perhaps if the horse develops a sudden inexplicable vice such as bucking or rearing, which may also give rise to an uncharacteristic change of temperament or performance.

Chiropractic can be used as part of an overall healthcare plan for your horse but it is not intended to replace traditional veterinary medicine. It certainly has a role in preventive healthcare, and is widely used in the racing industry where much of the equine chiropractor's work is in trying to enable the horses to remain healthy in order that they may continue their work programmes without unexpected interruptions. Horses are treated after falls over the jumps or on a regular, preventive basis on the flat.

MASSAGE THERAPY

Just as humans suffer from stress and tension, so do horses. In time, such conditions will start to affect performance and health. The pressures of competition are far greater for horses competing at higher levels and such horses are often pushed to the limits to obtain ultimate fitness and stamina. After a time they may start to become tense and uptight, and their performance starts to suffer unless some form of release is offered. This is where massage can help: it is the purposeful manipulation of muscle, ligaments and joints which is carried out in order to develop elasticity, circulation and range of motion within tissue. Generally it has a calming and relaxing effect and helps to remove stiffness by offering gentle, progressive relief. However, those who are experienced in massage techniques can achieve far greater results, not least by allaying old muscle injuries that impede free motion.

There are many different techniques used. The Tellington-Jones Equine Awareness Method (TEAM), which is based on relaxation and understanding between horse and rider or handler, aims to create a unique trust between the two. The technique is simple to learn and any combination of horse and rider or handler can benefit. Its philosophy indicates that a physically and mentally relaxed horse is more able to carry out what is asked.

CASE HISTORY

SHAMROCK: 16.00 hh palomino gelding, 13 years old. This horse is used for long distance riding events. He is extremely fit and his body is highly tuned. In order to prevent health problems, his owner gives him an all over massage before, during and after competitions. He often stiffens up on the day after a competition and so he is given a massage with aromatic oils and left to rest. The following day he is back to normal. His owner pays attention to every aspect of his health and with the aid of massage he has given her four years of loyal service. He is still going strong.

An unhappy horse never performs well and often starts to fight his rider.

When performed correctly, massage can help soft tissue and muscular problems. For instance, blood flow can be increased in a repairing area by relieving muscle spasm and releasing tension. Massage also takes away pain because it releases natural pain killing substances called endorphines. Any dedicated horse owner can learn the art of massage, but it would be unwise to go ahead without first consulting a specialist who can offer professional advice and a trained eye.

The trained masseur's fingers can pick up sensitive areas by identifying tension in the tissues underneath the skin. Similarly muscle spasm can be detected which indicates a disturbance to the structures upon which the muscle acts, or to the muscle itself.

While the horse owner can learn massage techniques which will improve the horse's well-being, by toning and relaxation, a veterinary diagnosis is required where there is any sign of illness or lameness. This is also true for the masseur; like other therapies, it is for the veterinary surgeon to diagnose and the healthcare professional (in this case the masseur) to treat the condition on the basis of the diagnosis given. If massage is administered before a diagnosis has been reached, it may do more harm than good as it may only be treating the effect, not the cause. For example, your horse seems stiff in his near shoulder and you decide to massage this area. The vet arrives, examines the horse and announces that there is a problem in the offside knee. The horse has overcompensated for pain felt in the knee by putting most of the weight on to the nearside limb, which caused tension and spasm in the nearside shoulder.

Massage techniques used by the horse owner

There is a growing interest among horse owners in how to massage correctly and effectively. Many appreciate that massage can be used to warm horses up before competition, to relax them after competition or within their normal routine, and to aid both their mental and physical well-being, giving them an overall sense of vitality.

The best way of learning how to massage correctly is to go to a trained physiotherapist who has been practising equine massage for some time. They may not be willing to show you the more professional techniques, as these require a considerable understanding of the horse's anatomy, muscles, ligaments and joints and how they all interact with one another, but most are willing to show you some techniques that will benefit a horse's overall health.

In days gone by you could have learned many such techniques from an experienced groom, who looked upon a 'good old strapping' as an essential part of the horse's grooming requirements. He would have combined such massage techniques with a sensible

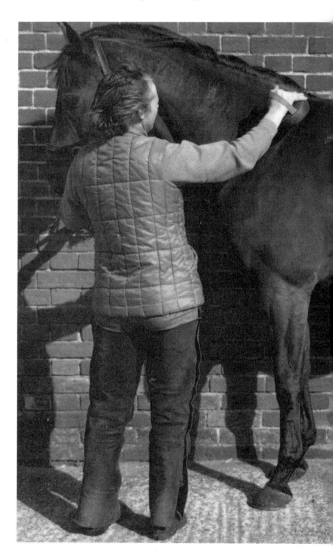

exercise and feeding programme to maintain the optimum physical efficiency of the horses in his care. Sadly today, most of us have far less time for our horses than we would like and such methods, as a matter of routine, have largely disappeared.

The relatively passive massages that owners will be able give their horses will help to relax them by increasing the circulation and easing any muscle spasm. Initially horses might seem to resent the massage until they get used to the new sensation, and so a little reassurance may be needed at first. All parts of the body can be massaged, from the tail to

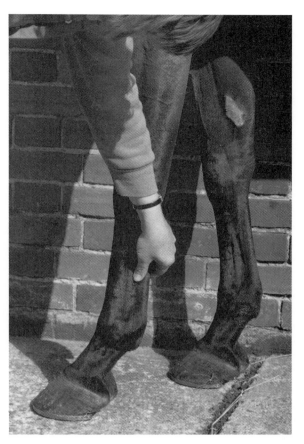

Most riders 'nip down' the horse's tendons after a ride without realizing that they are providing a valuable massage.

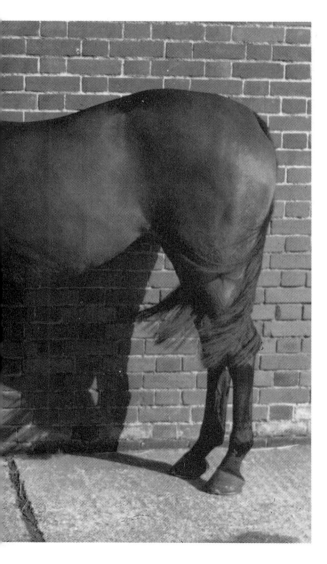

A 'good old strapping' used to be an essential part of the horse's grooming requirements.

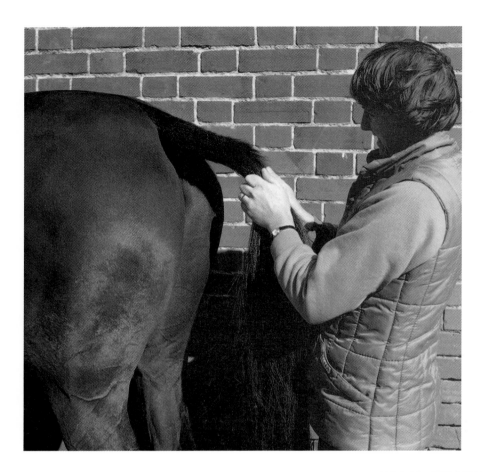

Even the tail can be massaged with beneficial effects.

The thumbs are moved in a circular fashion, stretching the skin outwards and upwards as they go.

the ears, and after the initial sessions most hors learn to anticipate a massage.

Getting to know your horse's reactions is the k to successful massage. You will soon acquire a sensitivity towards those reactions, which will enable you to assess the situation. If there is any tension or soreness you will be able to feel it, though you may not be able to see it.

When massaging large areas such as the rump and shoulders, most owners use a pushing and pulling motion with a slightly cupped hand. The idea is to use just enough pressure to move the underlying muscles; fast, heavy movements are not necessary. Smaller areas can be massaged by using a circular movement with the fingertips.

The thumbs also play a part in massage and are effective when used on the lower legs. The thumbs are also moved in a circular fashion, stretching the

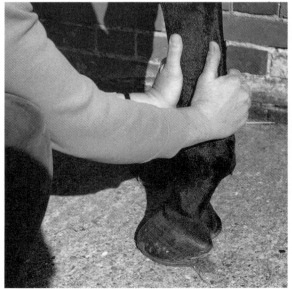

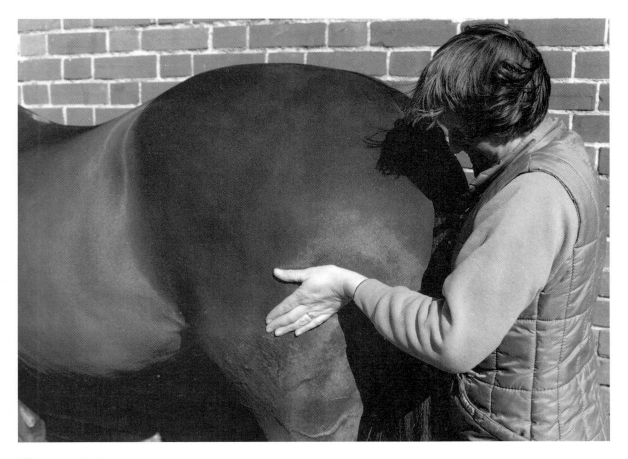

When massaging large areas such as the rump and shoulders, most owners use a pushing and pulling motion with a lightly cupped hand.

skin outwards and upwards as they go. When massaging the legs always work from the bottom upwards as this encourages venous return.

Unless headshy, many horses seem to appreciate having their ears massaged and many lower their heads in anticipation of the pleasure. This can be accomplished by working the fingertips in a rolling motion from the base along to the tips of the ears. The ears can then also be moved gently in wide circular movements.

There are many ways to give massage and as long as the sessions are approached sensibly, in a relaxed manner, both horse and owner can benefit. The

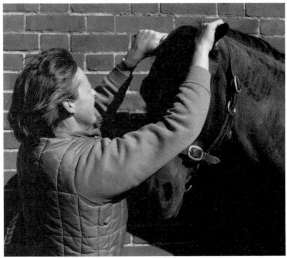

The ears can be moved gently in wide circular movements.

bond between an individual horse and owner or rider is always important and massage helps to form and maintain such a bond by providing a close and pleasurable contact between the two.

Techniques used by the professional physiotherapist

Hand massage is an art. While trained physiotherapists can learn the techniques needed to be effective, they also need to have a 'feel' for it. Professional masseurs can help to increase circulation, influence lymphatic flow and reduce pain. Their task is to find any defective areas, through sense and touch, and restore them to normal functioning.

Circulatory flow

The pumping action of the horse's heart achieves a circulatory flow of blood around the body. This ensures that oxygen, and other components of blood, reach the places where they are needed. If circulation is sluggish, oxygen will be not be received quickly enough where it is needed, which can have an effect on performance.

The horse's temperature is also controlled by the circulatory system. When the body temperature rises or falls, the circulatory flow reacts so as to reduce or increase temperature. The blood vessels are able to contract to generate heat where needed, or are able to dilate and lose heat through the skin.

When an injury occurs the horse's circulation helps to bring the body's necessary defence forces to the damaged site and will also carry away any unwanted matter. Therefore, circulatory flow has an impact on healing, so increasing the flow by massage will help to aid the quality of repair.

Lymphatic flow

The lymphatic system controls the flow of lymph through the body. Lymph is a clear fluid that contains water, protein, fat and a small number of white blood cells (lymphocytes). It is linked to the circulatory system in that it removes all waste products from it, acting as a filter system. However, its main task is to keep the body's defence and immunity system in order, which is of course all important in times of injury or illness.

Lymphatic flow is naturally very sluggish and if the horse is idle due to an injury or illness then movement of the lymph through the system slows even more, although injury increases the amount of fluid present at the site of the damage. In such cases massage can help to maintain the horse's muscle activity which will improve the movement of lymph through the system, so keeping the defending cells of the body in order.

Pain reduction

The body has its own natural pain relieving substances called endorphins, which are produced by the nervous system. Massage applied to a painful area acts as a trigger to the brain to release the endorphins, which will offer some pain relief. In turn the horse's muscles will relax, which will then enable the body's transport systems (circulation and lymphatic flow) to function normally.

Massage strokes

The trained physiotherapist will use three main massage strokes, each having its own purpose: effleurage, petrissage and friction. Such massage techniques are very hard work, although it is really technique rather than muscle power which is needed. When first evaluating the situation, experienced physiotherapists will be able to ascertain what technique to use from the feel of the tissues lying underneath the skin. They will be able to judge, from the reaction in the tissues, how well the muscles are responding to the technique being used, and they should be prepared to alter the technique if necessary. The therapist's stance, hand and finger pressure and frame of mind will all have an effect on the quality of the massage being applied.

While a veterinary surgeon should have already made a diagnosis if there is a problem with the horse, and directed the physiotherapist to treat the condition, the physiotherapist may have to refer the horse back to the vet if an abnormal reaction is experienced.

There are some contraindications to massage, especially those techniques which are deep in their action, which is why they should only be carried out by those who are trained or experienced.

Effleurage

Effleurage is an informing stroke, which will provide the physiotherapist with vital information about what is going on under the skin's surface. In a rhythmical way the physiotherapist will apply an inward and downward pressure away from and back towards her or his body, to the extent of the area being treated. The contact is a light one which may increase in pressure over areas of muscle. Usually the horse will be treated for no less than 10 or 15 minutes, when the physiotherapist may go on to use another technique. It can be performed with only the fingers or thumb; with the whole of the hand or just the heel of the hand, or with the fist, knuckles, elbow or forearm.

The technique is a good one to use as a warm up to competition or another type of massage, or as a cool down after exertion or following a different type of massage. It can also be used to calm an anxious horse; to reduce oedema (swelling) at the site of an injury; or to offer relief from pain due to muscle spasm. Depending on the problem, the pressure applied can be deep (great) or superficial (slight) or a combination of the two.

When rhythmically grooming your horse with a body brush and curry comb to 'bring out the shine', you are in effect giving a type of effleurage massage, as long as the strokes are purposeful and not weak. The type of grooming machines which have revolving heads also perform a type of effleurage, although they should be used with care as manes and tails can easily become entangled.

Petrissage

The physiotherapist will often use this technique to limit muscle tension after a period of exertion, helping to promote localized circulation. When used in conjunction with effleurage it can be very beneficial in controlling muscle tone after joint injuries and also helps the muscles to dispense with any waste products produced as a result of exertion.

The physiotherapist will use either the whole hands or just the fingers, depending on the desired result. The technique involves taking hold of the muscle belly (the bulk of the muscle) then pushing firmly down before lifting up as if to hold the muscle in the palm of the hands while applying a gentle stretching motion, before relaxing and repeating.

You can perform a type of petrissage stroke by using a strapping pad. The muscle is squeezed when you apply the pad and then released when you remove the pad. The pressure needs to be firm, but the horse does not need to be 'slapped' with the pad in the traditional way. Strapping, in conjunction with correct exercise and feeding is still an excellent way of toning the horse up but is often overlooked in preference for more modern methods.

Friction

Friction is a much more intense stroke, where improvement to a specific damaged area is sought. The stroke is deep and precise and needs to be performed by the trained hand, as an inexperienced one could cause further damage. Once learned correctly, the trained physiotherapist can use the technique for many things including breaking down adhesions and scar tissue and in the treatment of ruptured tendons or ligaments.

Friction is applied locally by the forefinger of one hand, reinforced by the second finger, being moved over the area with deep sweeping movements across the fibres. The piece of underlying tissue is moved backwards and forwards which results in the breakdown of scar tissue and adhesions.

7 ACUPUNCTURE

Competitors are always looking for ways of keeping their horses healthy without contravening the rules of each competitive discipline or the rules of racing. Acupuncture is a safe complementary therapy in that it offers a drug-free alternative, which is one of the reasons why its popularity is increasing among competitors and owners.

In the most limited sense, acupuncture is the insertion of fine sterile needles into specific points of the horse's body. Its purpose is to produce physiological responses, which will enable a self-healing process to take effect. It has been used to treat a variety of equine conditions and while it is not a panacea for all illnesses, many horses respond to treatment fairly well. Modern research has shown that acupuncture can affect most of the body systems: it is especially useful for arthritis, back pain, chronic catarrh, injuries involving ligaments, tendons and muscles and any chronic pain which is not being controlled by conventional treatment or when side effects are a problem.

Until there is specific training for those who want to become 'qualified acupuncturists', only qualified veterinary surgeons, with experience in the field, should perform acupuncture. As with other complementary treatments, acupuncture can be used as an accessory to traditional veterinary techniques, especially when taking care of the overall health of

In the most limited sense, acupuncture is the insertion of fine sterile needles into specific points of the horse's body.

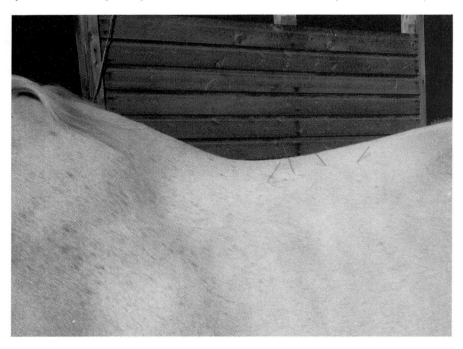

An acupuncture needle. When it is inserted into specific points of the horse's body it will provoke a physiological response.

the horse, but acupuncture diagnosis is not meant to be used as a substitute for a conventional veterinary diagnosis.

Acupuncture-type treatments were thought to exist about 6000–7000 years ago in India. Acupuncture as we know it today is a form of treatment developed some three or four thousand years ago in China. Its basis, and indeed that of traditional Chinese medicine, is that a life energy (**CHI** or **QI**) consisting of the eternal opposites **Yang** (positive) and **Yin** (negative) flows through the body in channels known as **meridians**. These channels run close to the surface of the body at specific points, known as **acupuncture points**. The ancient Chinese believed that illness is a state of imbalance or blockage in the normal energy flows of the body and that acupuncture restored them to normal by acting on the channels of energy flow.

An acupuncturist considers the body as an energetic whole. While a regular flow of energy through the meridians is maintained in a constant 24-hour cycle, with a balance between Yang and Yin components, all is well. It is when the energy flow is disturbed or obstructed that signs of disease become apparent. Disease is therefore simply considered to be an imbalance of the body's energy which causes a departure from harmony, and thus health.

Such Chinese philosophy is far removed from the Western way of thinking and this is perhaps why such treatments are often viewed sceptically. However, recent studies into the physiology of acupuncture have produced an understanding in Western medical terms of its mode of action.

THE ACUPUNCTURIST'S VIEW

To understand the treatment of horses by acupuncture, you need to realize that the acupuncturist sees the equine body as a self-healing entity. However, self-healing can be restrained if the body's energy is unbalanced. At such times the acupuncturist will work to re-establish normal energy levels by stimulating specific acupuncture points. Once this has been accomplished, self-healing can commence. In stark contrast, conventional medicine is inclined to treat specific symptoms which, if suppressed, may

CASE HISTORY

JACKSON: 16.3 hh eventer, 7 years old. This horse had recently been purchased but never performed up to expectations. The owner eventually noticed that he became overheated and did not perspire when other competing horses were sweating profusely. This resulted in the horse tiring quickly.

On examination it was found that the horse's cooling mechanism was not working properly. To promote correct heat dispersal, two acupuncture treatments were given at an interval of a week. Since the last treatment the horse has sweated normally after vigorous exercise and has not shown signs of early fatigue as previously.

mask the actual illness. For example, it is possible to relieve a high temperature, but there must be some underlying condition which caused the high temperature in the first place.

It is somewhat unfortunate that an acupuncturist may only be called in as a last resort, after conventional veterinary treatment has failed to give any significant results. The disease or illness is then far more advanced and the self-healing process will take longer to take effect. Undoubtedly, many horses for whom acupuncture is an option would benefit from earlier treatment.

Acupuncture treatment in the horse is usually by the insertion of needles into appropriate points, very often enhanced by electro-acupuncture, especially in painful conditions. Low-intensity or cold beam lasers are sometimes used as a means of stimulating points, largely because the procedure is painless and does not take as long to perform. The laser is used to treat specific conditions via the acupuncture points, rather than directly treating the affected area. However, the laser beam can only penetrate a short distance into the tissue and therefore is of limited value in heavily muscled areas. Stimulation to the points can also be provided by massage with the

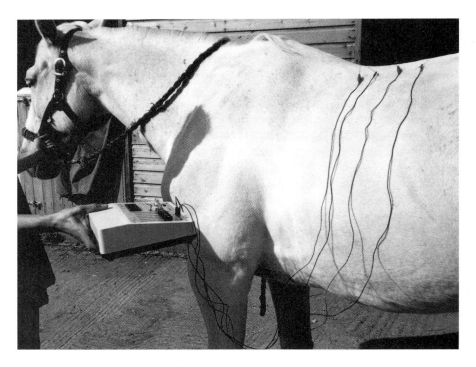

Electro-acupuncture is often used to induce the body's own pain relieving substances.

fingers (**acupressure**), electrical currents, implant or injection, or by **moxibustion** which is the heating of specific acupuncture points by burning Moxa (a herb) above or on the skin over them.

Electro-acupuncture is used to induce the body's own pain-relieving substances. The acupuncturist can control the voltage, increasing it gradually until the desired effect is seen – usually a bunching of the muscles. Most horses tolerate this type of stimulus well and the method is an extremely valuable one for acupuncture analgesia prior to surgery.

There are other methods of stimulation although they are not used as extensively and some are only used very occasionally. The **implant technique** is used when extended stimulation of the points is required. Various materials, such as gold or surgical staples, can be 'implanted' by means of a large-gauge hypodermic needle at acupuncture points to produce extreme localized swelling. Some cases of navicular disease are said to have been treated favourably by this technique.

Other forms of injection techniques include aquapuncture and pneumo-acupuncture. **Aquapuncture** is the use of hypodermic needles to inject a

CASE HISTORY

JENNY: 16.2 hh bay hunter mare, 8 years old. This horse was said to feel 'tight' behind the saddle. She was reluctant to bend to the right and did not track up properly with short strides and a tendency to stumble behind at the walk. Examination revealed tenderness and tension in the upper lumbar area of the bladder meridian.

Electro-acupuncture was carried out on eight acupuncture points and laser treatment was given on two further points.

The horse was re-examined two weeks later when the owner reported a considerable degree of improvement.

Treatment was repeated; the horse was re-examined one week later and reported to be performing normally. The treatment was repeated again and the horse has behaved normally ever since which is now two years from the last treatment.

substance (which may be a simple saline solution or vitamin B_{12} or even a homoeopathic remedy) under the skin at the specific points. The principle is that the pressure created by the solution stimulates the point for about ten or fifteen minutes.

Pneumo-acupuncture is used occasionally, most often for problems in the horse's shoulder. Instead of a substance or foreign body being injected, air is inserted under the skin. This forms a 'pocket' which is manipulated downward until it has dispersed.

In effect, even **twitching** the horse's upper lip is a form of acupuncture. The twitch has a restraining and calming effect because it releases encephalins and endorphins (morphine-like substances) from the brain.

ACUPUNCTURE POINTS

An acupuncture point is an area of the skin which has a greater density of neuroreceptors than surrounding areas. Pathological conditions lead to an increased vascular permeability and lowered electrical resistances at these points, augmenting their sensitivity. These tender points or trigger points may be produced by muscle spasm, tensions or endocrine imbalance.

Most acupuncture points are described as lying on meridians or channels which connect with other acupuncture points and have functional relationships with them. Traditionally each acupuncture point has one or several actions when stimulated and when used in combination with other points the results are modified.

There are three types of acupuncture point. The main ones are located along the paths of large nerves in the skin and muscle. Secondary ones are found in smaller nerves, while the third type are located at small nerves running through the muscle.

Acupuncture can also be used as a diagnostic aid, whereby the acupuncturist assesses the reactions given from finger stimulation to certain 'association' points. These points may be very important to the treatment of a condition, as well as its diagnosis and each specific point has an express link with a meridian and an internal organ. Down each side of the spine certain acupuncture points are related to internal organs and to certain parts of the limbs. However, pain at these points does not necessarily

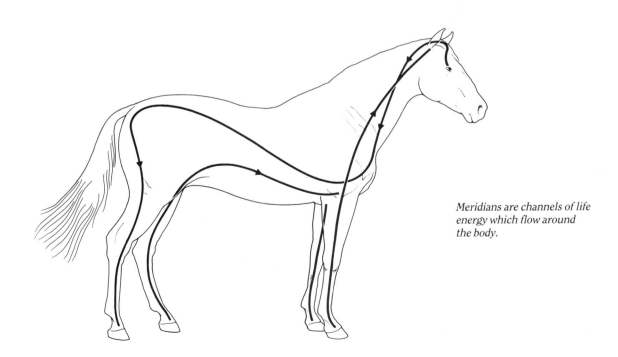

Meridians are channels of life energy which flow around the body.

mean that the seat of the trouble is at the painful point but that the pain is referred from an internal organ or from one of the limbs. The experienced acupuncturist can evaluate the reactions given and therefore make an informed diagnosis.

How it Works

The site of a specific problem may be far away from the acupuncture point which is stimulated to produce an effect. For example, precisely defined points situated on the body surface down each side of the spine are related to their own specific internal organ or organ system. There are twelve main meridians on each side of the body with precisely defined acupuncture points, and each location will correspond to a specific part of the horse's body. Pain located near a specific acupuncture point will indicate to the acupuncturist that there may be disease in the corresponding organ.

Destructive influences, which may be effects of poor nutrition, emotional pressures, traumatic incidents, climatic conditions or more simply pressure from ill-fitting saddlery or incompetent riding, have an impact on the body via the meridians, which can affect the body's organs and systems. Some points correspond to the limbs and may therefore be important in diagnosing and treating lameness and similarly with back complaints.

If we understand these principles we can begin to see how acupuncture may be appropriate for internal disease as well as painful conditions such as those which cause lameness or back trouble. More specifically, COPD, colic, laminitis and skin diseases have been known to respond well. The acupuncturist can do much to alleviate these conditions, but will also ensure that the owner is aware of the need to manage the condition properly and prevent it from recurring if possible.

Like any form of medicine, one course of acupuncture will not provide a miracle cure. While it can have rapid effects, a long-term view will be more beneficial. The horse owner has a duty to manage the horse in a responsible and caring manner, ensuring correct feeding, shoeing, saddling and so on, and thus preventing many of the detrimental influences on the horse's body in the first place.

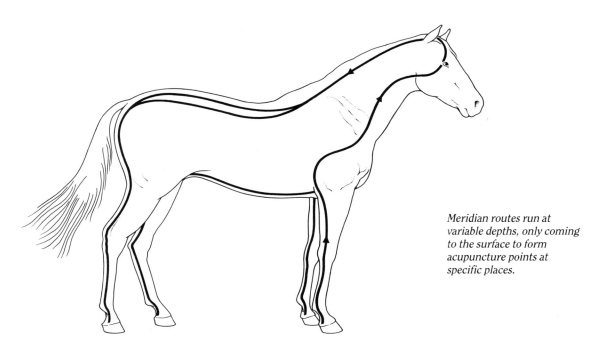

Meridian routes run at variable depths, only coming to the surface to form acupuncture points at specific places.

CLINICAL SIGNS WHICH MAY RESPOND TO ACUPUNCTURE

Poll and cervical
Head carriage tilted
Shaking of the head
Inability to turn head on neck
Heavy discharge from one nostril after exercise
Jaw-cocking on turns and/or inability to flex down

Withers, saddle and rib angles
Inability to turn from shoulders
Hopping into trot on a circle
Shortness of stride in front
Dislike of girth being tightened
Dislike of being mounted
Irritability in temperament
Stiffness on one rein

Lumbar
Disunited at canter
Changing legs at canter
Not wanting to bend on a given leg
Bucking
Dislike of mounting
Refusing at jumps, especially from a turn
Napping when saddling and mounting
Dipping when being mounted
Irritability in temperament
Stiffness on one rein

Sacroiliac
Dragging hind limb/s
Knocking out toes of shoes (squaring off)
Going close behind and knocking pasterns/fetlocks
Going wide behind
Cold back
Not going forward
Unlevel on the lunge
Difficult to shoe behind
Loss of muscle bulk in pelvis/hind limb
Bucking on transitions (e.g. trot into canter)
Rolling

WHAT TO EXPECT

Acupuncturists will firstly ask about the horse. They will want to know about the horse's normal behaviour and what has been happening to make you call upon their services. If you are ever thinking about acupuncture as a treatment, keep a day-by-day record of your horse's symptoms and behaviour to aid the acupuncturist in treating the condition.

Secondly, acupuncturists will give the horse a thorough examination from the tip of the nose to the base of the tail, observing and feeling as they go. Particular attention will be paid to the horse's head, spine, underside of the neck and the site of injury or disease. They will then ask for the horse to be trotted up, if he is able, looking for signs of imbalance: the horse carrying the head or tail to one side, for example. They will then ask to see the horse in a certain situation which, if their instincts are right, will probably make the horse worse. For instance, if a horse has a suspected problem with a certain limb but appears sound, the acupuncturist may ask for him to be turned in a tight circle to see if lameness becomes apparent.

Acupuncturists decide how best to treat horses on the basis of the history of the horse's condition and on their own observations. If needles are to be used, these will be inserted and left in place for a measured time. Most horses seem to accept the treatment quite readily and some even doze while the treatment is being given.

If acupuncture is going to work for an individual horse, the response will be fairly quick. Beneficial effects can often be seen within three or four treatments if it is going to be successful. Any techniques used should be selected for individual needs with the support of internal medicine and nutrition, with the use of herbs and perhaps with homoeopathy. It is not sufficient simply to locate an acupuncture point, stick in a needle and hope for the best; the whole aim is to stimulate the body's own healing powers. It cannot be stressed enough, then, that acupuncture should not and cannot be practised by the layman. A great understanding of the equine body and much observation of the horse is a prerequisite for the acupuncturist.

The horse has a highly developed sensitivity, is extremely sensitive to pain and is also said to have developed the best sixth sense of all animals. It is probably because of these reasons that almost 100% of horses will respond to a greater rather than lesser extent to acupuncture and acupressure. Where a horse seems resentful to the use of needles, acupressure may be more suitable. In many cases it is the more highly bred types that seem resentful, which in practice is unfortunate as they also seem to respond the best.

Contacting an equine acupuncturist

At present only a small number of acupuncturists specialize in equines. Because of its increasing popularity, there is a danger that people may set themselves up as acupuncturists when they have no more right to be one than you or I. It is therefore safer to ensure that any acupuncturist treating your horse is a proper veterinary operator by contacting the appropriate professional association (see Useful Addresses).

If you do not observe this fundamental rule, you could be left with a crippled horse and no redress. Only proper veterinary acupuncturists are able to insure themselves against negligence and only they are able to diagnose the best possible treatment for your horse.

CASE HISTORIES

CODY: 15 hh chestnut, Thoroughbred gelding, 14 years old. This horse had severe laminitis in both fore feet, and was treated using the hoof wall resection technique. After two years the horse was able to be ridden and had competed at local dressage competitions, where he was placed on several occasions.

He then had two consecutive outings on harder ground and got the comment 'stiff in the loins' both times. Although there was no evidence of bruising or spasm in the back muscles it was thought appropriate to see whether the stiffness could be alleviated with acupuncture. After a single treatment, his usual rider, who did not know of the treatment, was amazed that the horse was much more supple in his back, particularly in corners and seemed to have no difficulty cantering on the left leg, which up to then had always been a problem.

BARNABY: 16.1 hh bay gelding, 16 years old. This horse had been hunted and then used as a weight carrier in a riding school. He came into private hands when the riding school closed down, and the owner became aware that the horse was deteriorating in his movements. He was diagnosed, using scintigraphy and X-rays, as having navicular disease, bone spavin, two impingeing dorsal spinous processes and an old cruciate ligament tear.

The first acupuncture treatment enabled him to use his back muscles so effectively that by flexing his loins and quarters he is more than able to compensate for arthritic stiffness in the hocks, and any weakness in the stifle. He had four acupuncture treatments to reduce any muscle tensions which may have accumulated through guarding stiff joints and is ridden every day with no apparent discomfort.

8 HERBS FOR HORSES

Herbalism is the use of certain plants, either internally or externally, to effect a remedy for varied conditions, or to provide essential nutrients lacking in the horse's diet. Throughout the 16th and 17th centuries, plants formed the basis of many equine treatments, and it is only in the last century that synthetic drugs have been developed and become widely used – in fact to such an extent that the use of herbs has declined rapidly.

Years ago herbalism was an accepted practice amongst stable staff. The head lad would likely have learnt from his predecessor, often his father, how and what to use for a desired outcome. There were no scientific reasons to back up the knowledge passed on and undoubtedly such insight evolved through trial and error. If the horse became ill, the lad would know not to use a certain herb for the same condition next time. Certain individuals gained great wisdom in the use of herbs and unquestionably this would have been their best kept secret. It is because of this that an element of mystery and superstition surrounded the use of herbs. Those who could use them expertly were known as 'herbalists' by people who believed in their use, and as 'cranks' by those who did not.

Nowadays the use of herbs is very popular again, not only with the average horse owner but also with some members of the veterinary profession. We have an advantage over our predecessors in that we can make extensive use of scientific apparatus and techniques to analyse the properties of various plants, which will inform us how they may affect the horse's body and health. While there is still not much in the way of actual scientific research into the use of herbs for certain conditions, there is a tremendous amount of feedback to herbal manufacturers and interaction between horse owners, whose observations provide useful statistics. It is now acknowledged that herbs are valuable for both nutritional and medical therapy.

It is important to realize though, that herbs are not an elixir for every condition. There are cases where a herbal remedy will not be the most appropriate form of treatment so it is wise to consult a veterinary surgeon or experienced herbal practitioner before proceeding to treat an illness. Ensure that the herbal practitioner has experience of herbal remedies for horses, as some human remedies may be harmful. If in any doubt whatsoever, consult a veterinary surgeon before continuing as there are many natural potentially toxic substances.

HERBS VS CONVENTIONAL MEDICINES

Various conventional drugs have their origins in herbs; for example, aspirin originated from willow or meadowsweet, and morphine derivatives stemmed from the opium poppy. What then, is the real difference between conventional and natural medicine? The principle behind modern drug treatment is that a single active ingredient is used to treat the symptom. The principle behind herbalism is holism: a 'whole plant', which has properties that work together, is used to treat the 'whole patient' and so eliminate the *causes* of the symptoms.

When treating the symptoms alone, the underlying causes may still remain and recur, but when treating the whole body, a selection of herbs can be used in combination to achieve a harmonizing effect within the individual.

WHY FEED HERBS?

For deficiencies
Herbs contain a wide variety of balanced nutrients and chemicals, which can be beneficial because the

horse's demand for nutrients rises as his system demands increase. However, they should not be fed to such an extent that an imbalance occurs. Once the horse's system is receiving all the nutrients it requires, an excess of herbs will simply upset the system, not improve it. The greatest use of herbs in the nutritional sense is when a horse is known to be deficient of something. Following a correct diagnosis, the horse owner then has the opportunity of choosing a natural supplement from a biological plant source to balance the horse's system. In common with other complementary therapies, this requires an examination and diagnosis to be made by a veterinary surgeon in the first instance. Without a correct diagnosis you may be treating your horse improperly, which will delay correct treatment. Feeding herbs takes a little common sense, patience and a degree of observation and monitoring.

For performance horses

Another benefit of feeding herbs is that they do not contravene any rules of governing bodies for certain disciplines. This is especially useful for performance horses as with the aid of herbs they can often cope with a strenuous workload without suffering ill effects. The effect of herbs is a cumulative one and it takes time for them to act on the horse's system before the full benefits can be appreciated. Proprietary brands will give an indication of how much to add to the horse's feed but, as always, each horse is an individual and may need more or less than the stated amount.

THE MISSING ELEMENT

Before domestication, horses used to roam over vast areas of grasslands. In their travels they would find a variety of plants to satisfy their nutritional needs. They instinctively selected those plants which would be beneficial, both as sustenance and to aid recovery from illness – they seemed to have an innate 'dowsing' ability to find herbal remedies. As they became domesticated, they were restricted to grazing in fenced areas, and their natural feeding pattern was denied them. Herbs became a missing element.

Today the picture is largely the same and current feeding practices are often inappropriate. Horses are 'trickle' feeders, which means that naturally they feed constantly – 'little and often'. Stabled horses are usually put on to a 'three meals a day' regime. This does not correspond with their natural trickle feeding pattern, in which small amounts of food pass almost constantly through the digestive system, and this is one of the contributing factors to the bouts of colic from which many horses suffer.

A better system, and one which would not be too hard to implement would be to allow as much good quality hay as the horse could eat, with the addition of a concentrate ration when needed. The horse should only need extra nourishment if put into work, and then it should be built up gradually in line with the workload and fitness. However, while an ad lib supply of good quality hay can go a long way to feeding horses more naturally, it still does not provide the variety of grasses and herbs that they would eat if left to their own devices.

The increasing world interest in environmental issues has encouraged an upsurge in feeding herbs to horses and in the main this has been implemented in one of two ways: by adding herbs to pasture seed-mixes, and by adding them to the feed of stabled horses.

The horse at grass

Many permanent, untreated pastures retain their numerous and varied grasses and herbs, but sadly many horse owners do not recognize their worth and set about removing them to produce a nice 'clean' paddock of lush green grass. A few species, such as dandelions and nettles which are rich in minerals, will continue to appear and horses are often seen picking at these. However, few horse paddocks supply a selection of different herbs unless the horse owner provides them.

Where a horse is kept at grass for most of the time, a herb strip can be sown in the paddock. At the same time the paddock can be re-seeded with mixed seed containing beneficial varieties of grasses and herbs. Grasses are particularly low in minerals and their health-giving properties are limited, and so grass seed should be mixed with herbs to remedy the deficits. Chicory and plantain are two mineral-rich

Dandelions are mineral-rich;
they draw nutrients from
deep in the subsoil.

herbs that might be incorporated into a re-seeding mixture for the paddock. To find the correct grass/herb ratio for your paddock, contact the nearest agricultural advisory service to discover what is best for the local soil and climate.

When out at grass horses will ingest the fresh herbs as part of everyday grazing, which should help to prevent disease and generally keep them in good health. Domesticated horses have no opportunity to 'dowse' for their own remedies and have no choice but to leave their health in our care.

The stabled horse

Stable-kept horses, unable to browse herbs in a paddock, need them to be added to their feed.

Collected herbs can either be fed fresh, or dried for later use. Many companies produce herbal supplements for a given purpose and these are often more convenient for the busy horse owner who has no time for harvesting herbs. Most companies produce mixes for different types of horses – competition horses or in-foal mares, for example – as well as mixes prepared for a given purpose, perhaps as a fly repellent, or to aid good hoof strength.

Although uncommon, vitamin deficiencies are more likely to be found in the stable-kept horse than in one kept on grass, especially if the horse is denied access to green food and adequate sunshine. There is a danger that such deprivations will lead to a shortage of vitamins A and D.

Nettles provide a good source of protein and iron and have long been recognized for their beneficial effects upon the condition of the horse's coat.

HERBS FOR USE IN FEED

	Comfrey	Chicory	Clover	Dandelion	Fenugreek	Golden Rod	Garlic	Kelp	Linseed	Mint	Nettle	Raspberry	Rose hips	Brewers' yeast
Wounds and cuts	✓													
Sprains and strains	✓													
Fractures and broken bones	✓						✓							
Arthritis and rheumatism	✓					✓								
Anti-flatulent										✓				
Fattening			✓	✓					✓					
Conditioning		✓	✓	✓	✓	✓		✓	✓		✓		✓	✓
Laminitis							✓				✓		✓	
Sweet itch and mange							✓				✓			
C.O.P.D.							✓							
Colds and coughs				✓			✓		✓					
Mares in foal	✓		✓	✓			✓	✓				✓	✓	
Growth and bones			✓				✓	✓			✓		✓	
Digestion		✓		✓			✓			✓	✓			
Tonic		✓		✓			✓			✓	✓			
Hoof strength and condition													✓	
Calmative													✓	

HERBS FOR EXTERNAL USE

	Arnica	Chamomile	Comfrey	Golden Rod	Garlic	Myrrh	Frankincense	Mugwort	Pennyroyal	Rosemary	Rue	Sage	Thyme	Witch Hazel	Wild Geranium
Sores and galls	✓		✓			✓	✓							✓	
Burns and stings		✓								✓				✓	
Bruises	✓	✓	✓											✓	
Bleeding	✓	✓	✓							✓				✓	
Wounds	✓	✓	✓							✓				✓	
Skin disorders						✓	✓	✓	✓	✓	✓	✓	✓		✓
Cleansing						✓	✓	✓	✓			✓	✓		✓
Strains and swellings	✓		✓											✓	
Poultices		✓	✓	✓										✓	
Astringent						✓	✓			✓	✓	✓	✓	✓	✓
Antiseptic				✓	✓	✓	✓					✓	✓	✓	
Fly repellent					✓			✓	✓		✓				
Anti-inflammatory				✓	✓	✓					✓	✓	✓	✓	

Chart of herbs for horses. (Reproduced by kind permission of Feedmark.)

DIRECTORY OF HERBS

Many of these herbs can be obtained dry from health-food shops or horse feed merchants. However, if you have a good, clean source of fresh herbs, then it is very satisfying to pick your own and dry them for future use. Always make certain that you know what you are picking and storing: consult a qualified specialist if in doubt. To avoid contamination from mould in storage, always ensure that the herbs are completely dry and then pack them in airtight containers or sealable polythene bags.

Alfalfa *(Medicago sativa)*
Also known as lucerne and now extensively fed as a forage crop, this provides an excellent alternative to hay. It is commonly fed to horses who need to put on condition as it has a high protein, vitamin and mineral content. It grows from 28–100 cm (11 in–3 ft) in height and has a lilac flower. It can be eaten either fresh or dried.

Arnica *(Arnica montana)*
This deciduous plant has fine hairs on the top surface of its leaves and large yellow flowers which emerge in midsummer. It is good for treating bruises, haematomas, sores and galls, bleeding, wounds, strains and swellings. It should only be applied externally, as it is poisonous if taken internally. It contains tannic acid, arnicin and mucilage.

Arnica.

Chamomile *(Matricaria chamomilla, Chamaemelum nobile)*
This pleasantly scented low-growing annual has white daisylike flowers which appear in midsummer. It contains calcium, calenduline and potassium; and azulen can be extracted from its fresh flowers.

Chamomile is useful for burns, stings, bruises, wounds, sweet itch or dermatitis, and bleeding and has antiseptic attributes. It can be applied externally as a poultice or made as a cream, or given in the horse's feed. It is said to have sedative properties, so is often fed to highly strung horses or those prone to nervous colic.

Chicory *(Chichorium intybus)*
This has flowers of white, pink and blue (the blue ones are more abundant) and its leaves are rough and pointed. It is used as a general conditioning tonic, helping to aid digestion and has been scientifically proven to have a beneficial effect on the liver. Many owners of performance horses use chicory as an aid to recovery from overwork and strain. It contains organic salts and calenduline, and is added to the feed or planted in the pasture.

Coltsfoot *(Tussilago farfara)*
This has an orange-yellow daisylike flower with a woody stem and a large, flat leaf. It is often used in human cough medicines and can similarly be given to horses. About 30 ml (1 fl oz) twice a day can be administered by squirting into the horse's mouth using a large, needle-less syringe, for as long as the horse is suffering.

Comfrey *(Symphytum officinale)*
This is one of the herbs commonly found in old permanent pastures and yet it is one which causes much debate as it has been associated with liver complaints when taken internally, so it should be used with caution under qualified advice. It is recognized by its fleshy leaves and stands about 1 m (3 ft) high.

Traditionally comfrey has always been known as a highly nutritious healing and conditioning herb. Due to the presence of allantoin and choline, it is a valuable external application, encouraging the healing of strains, wounds and other tissue damage. It has been renowned for mending bones and as a result is often referred to as 'knitbone'. It can be applied using a poultice and some manufacturers sell these ready prepared.

Comfrey is also beneficial if taken internally, under guidance. In the daily feed it provides a valuable source of calcium, potassium, iron, vitamin B12, iodine and certain amino acids. When fed in this way it is said to help arthritis and rheumatism.

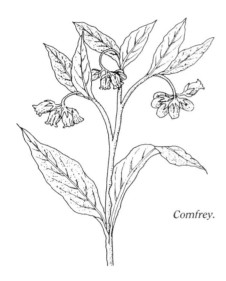

Comfrey.

Dandelion *(Taraxacum officinale)*
This is a common herb with long roots, toothed leaves and bright yellow flowers. It provides potassium, riboflavin, taraxacin, taraxerin, trace elements and vitamins B and C. The plant draws its own nutrients from deep in the subsoil and so is mineral rich. It is known for its qualities as a general conditioner and tonic. When eaten it stimulates the liver, kidneys and gall bladder and also has a slight laxative effect so helping to clear the body of waste matter and toxins. It has a history of use in the treatment of liver and urinary complaints.

Devil's Claw *(Harpagophytum procumbens)*
This has anti-inflammatory and pain-killing properties. It is an African plant but can bought dried from most herbal sources. It is often used initially to

relieve pain after injury, but has a longer term use in cases of arthritis.

Eucalyptus *(Eucalyptus globulus)*
This is a hanging plant with yellow feathery flowers. It is useful for catarrh but should be inhaled for best relief, which can be a little tricky with a fidgety horse. It can be bought in small bottles as Eucalyptus oil, which is easier to administer as a few drops can be put on a handkerchief and held underneath the horse's nostrils. If applied to the coat it will act as a fly repellent and is also said to help sprains.

Eyebright *(Euphrasia officinalis)*
This herb has pale lilac flowers and small toothed leaves and, as its name suggests it is used for the relief of sore eyes. It can be bought dried or as a tincture. An infusion can be made from the dried herbs and the eyes bathed twice daily.

Fenugreek *(Trigonella foenumgraecum)*
This herb has similar properties to linseed in that it contains oil and protein and is fed to fatten horses up. It is very palatable and is often used as an appetizer for faddy eaters. Additionally it is a good tonic as it is rich in vitamins, especially vitamin E. The seeds contain protein, mucilage, choline, flavone pigment, oils and lecithin.

Flax, linseed *(Linum usitatissimum)*
This plant can be recognized in farmers' fields as a blanket of light blue flowers. Individual plants grow up to 1.3 m (4 ft) in height and the leaves are very slim and spiky. The seeds (linseed) are the most useful part for herbal remedies: they contain about 40% oil and 25% protein and are an excellent 'fattener' and conditioner. However, they are poisonous if eaten raw; they must be boiled until they split and the mass resembles a jelly, which takes a minimum of two hours. Pure linseed oil is useful as a laxative but should be used sparingly – no more than 25–30 ml (about 1 fl oz) a day.

Frankincense *(Styrax benzion)*
Frankincense is the resin of a South East Asian tree, containing volatile oils and organic acids. It is

applied externally, usually as a tincture, as it has antiseptic, cleansing, astringent and anti-inflammatory effects.

Garlic *(Allium sativum)*

Garlic is probably one of the most widely used feed supplements. Its use and actions are many and varied. Firstly, it has a history of use in respiratory disorders. Horses suffering from allergies, coughs and colds will find relief from its expectorant and stimulant properties. Additionally it has been found beneficial:

- for horses prone to laminitis;
- as a fly repellent;
- in the control of sweet itch;
- for infection as an antibiotic;
- as a blood cleanser;
- in the reduction of worms;
- in cases of arthritis and rheumatism;
- in reducing blood cholesterol and blood pressure.

Its essential oils contain vitamins A, B2, B3 and C, sulphur, crontonaldehyde, minerals and trace elements. It is usually purchased as a convenient powder which is measured into the feed, but can also be supplied as a syrup or fed fresh. Pulped garlic can be valuable when applied externally as a poultice on infected wounds as it has antiseptic and anti-inflammatory powers.

Garlic.

Geranium, Wild *(Geranium maculatum)*

This perennial plant of North America has purple flowers in mid summer. It contains essential oils, organic acids, saponiside and tannin. It has astringent and styptic (a substance which checks bleeding) properties which make it an excellent foundation for a shampoo in the treatment of scurf and lice and as a repellent to mosquitos.

Golden Rod *(Solidago virgaurea)*

This native of Europe grows as a heathland or garden plant. It can grow up to 1.3 m (4 ft) high and has abundant golden flowers in late summer. It is found in many proprietary herbal mixes and contains essential oils, tannin, saponins and organic acids. It can be used internally to aid digestion, arthritis, rheumatism, promote appetite, as a mild diuretic and as a coat conditioner, or externally as a poultice to aid tissue healing.

Hops *(Humulus lupulus)*

This is cultivated in most parts of the world and is found as a climbing vine in Europe. Hops must not be eaten raw, but dried hops are a recognized sedative and pain relief. They are also used as a tonic and an aid to relieve stomach disorders; however, due to their sedative powers they should be used cautiously under specialist advice. They are not indicated for breeding stock as they have an effect on the hormonal system. Hops make an excellent tonic for the habitual worrier, and for the horse that becomes fractious when away from home.

Horseradish *(Cochlearia armoracia)*

Horseradish grows to 1 m (3 ft) and has a pungent odour. The root is normally found in the salad bowl, but is also valuable in herbal preparations. It can be used to promote the flow of blood to a repairing area and is prepared as a poultice. It can also be dried or prepared as an infusion and is said to promote perspiration and is also a diuretic. Horseradish can also be added to cough preparations.

Hyssop *(Hyssopus officinalis)*

This is found wild in the UK as a small field herb. It is used as a stimulant and carminative for bronchial and nasal catarrh; it can also be used for anxiety states and tension. It contains hysopine, organic compounds of iron and aromatic oils and can be used in the mild massage of bruises.

Kelp, seaweed (Fucus vesiculosus)

Often referred to as 'bladderwrack', this is the type of seaweed seen growing along the seashore. It is also readily available as dried kelp powder. It contains algin, B-caratene, iodine, calcium, potassium, volatile oils and other trace elements. It is used externally as a compress on rheumatic joints; or it can be dried and fed to old, fatigued or young horses as it provides a good source of dietary calcium. It also promotes a good healthy coat and strong hooves. It has a slight laxative action so can help in cases of flatulent colic.

CASE HISTORY

CANDY: 14.2 hh working hunter pony, 7 years old. This pony had excellent conformation, but unfortunately had brittle hooves which cracked easily. This often led to her being put down the line against lesser horses. She also seemed to suffer from bouts of flatulent colic soon after shows and occasionally during shows.

She was fed a mixture of herbs with a main ingredient of kelp. The first noticeable sign of improvement was the absence of flatulent colic after shows and as the weeks went on it became apparent that her hooves were growing more strongly, without cracking up. Her coat also bloomed and she looked the picture of health. She has gone on to win many classes, often against ponies to which she lost before.

Marigold (Calendula)

This is a common cultivated plant in many gardens with orange and yellow flowers. The petals contain calenduline, potassium and calcium and can be prepared as an infusion, a cream, a poultice or fed dried. They have anti-fungal, anti-inflammatory and antibacterial qualities and so are very beneficial in wound-healing. They are also used for liver conditions, digestive ailments, thrush, ringworm, mud fever, rain scald and cracked heels.

Mint (Mentha spicata – spearmint, Mentha piperata – peppermint)

This common garden herb is used to aid digestion and as an appetizer, and in cases of flatulent colic. Fresh mint, finely chopped and mixed into the feed, will encourage a faddy eater. Both species contain oils (menthol) which can be extracted and used as an inhalant. It is also useful in cases of ringworm as it has anti-fungal qualities.

Mint.

Mugwort (Artemisia absinthium)

This herb contains aromatic oils and is useful for the treatment of bruises. It can also be used as a fly repellent. It contains absinthine and mucilage.

Myrrh (Commiphora molmol)

Myrrh is a resin of an Arabian tree. Its uses are similar to those for Frankincense.

Nettle (Urtica dioica)

The nettle is considered to be a weed and therefore is all too often removed from paddocks. It is a good source of protein and iron and has long been recognized for its beneficial effect upon the condition of the coat. It also contains histamine and formic acid (this is what gives it its sting), tannin, vitamins, mineral and trace elements. It has been reported as a good appetizer when dried and added to the feed. Other beneficial effects include improvements in anaemia, sweet itch, rheumatism and laminitis (when combined with rosehips). It also has value as an anti-asthmatic.

Parsley *(Petroselinum crispum)*

This biennial has white flowers and aromatic leaves. It contains vitamins A, B and C, iron and other trace elements. It is useful as a diuretic in the treatment of kidney disorders and can aid digestion and relieve rheumatism.

Pennyroyal *(Mentha pulegium)*

This low-growing European herb contains pulergose and is used externally in the treatment of skin irritations and insect bites. Applied before turning out it can act as a fly repellent.

Plantain *(Plantago ginis)*

One of the herbs which can still be found in untreated permanent pastures this is mineral rich and in addition contains tannic acid and mucilage. It acts as a blood cleanser and can be used as a laxative.

Raspberry *(Rubus idaeus)*

This is probably the most common additive on studs as it is known to aid parturition in mares and fertility in stallions. The leaves contain fragrine which when used in the two months prior to foaling and directly after foaling, is beneficial in improving muscle tone and a good milk yield.

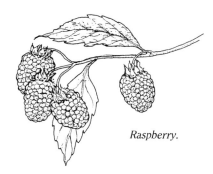

Raspberry.

Red Clover *(Trifolium pratense)*

Also known as trefoil, this herb is usually fed dried to promote a healthy coat and act as a general tonic. As it has sedative properties, it is sometimes fed to competition horses who 'hot up' before an event. It contains calcium, sugars, glucosides, essential oils and salicylic acid.

Rose *(Rosa canina)*

This plant is often referred to as the wild dog rose. The hips contain a valuable source of biotin for strong hoof growth. Hips and leaves also contain pectin, tannin, organic acids and vitamins, especially vitamin C. It is useful as a barrier against infection and as a general tonic and conditioner.

Rose Hips.

Rosemary *(Rosmarinus officinalis)*

This is a common cooking herb, readily available dried, and often grown in herb gardens. It contains tannin, bitterine and essential oils. It is useful in gastric disorders, as a carminative, nervine and tonic. When combined with southernwood it is said to aid hair growth.

Rue *(Ruta graveolens)*

This herb can cause allergic reactions in those preparing it and should only be used with specialist advice. It contains aromatic oil, bitterine and albumin. Most often used as an antiseptic wash when dealing with skin complaints or insect bites, it can also be used as a fly repellent.

Sage *(Salvia officinalis)*

This garden herb contains organic acids, volatile oils and tannins. It has uses as an anti-fungal, anti-inflammatory and as an astringent.

Southernwood *(Artemisia arbrotanum)*

This herb is mostly collected for its essential and volatile oils. It can be used as an antiseptic or a stimulant and is useful in restoring hair when blended with rosemary.

St John's wort *(Hypericum perforatum)*

This sturdy yellow-flowered herb should only be used externally. Prepared as a cream it can aid healing of wounds.

Thyme *(Thymus vulgaris)*

Widely available, this herb has small evergreen leaves; its small lilac flowers appear in May. It contains a powerful antiseptic (thymol) and also has anti-inflammatory and astringent properties. Can be used for coughs and bronchial conditions.

Valerian *(Valeriana officinalis)*

This small herb is excellent for relieving nervous tension on a short-term basis – when arriving at a new stables for instance. It can cause drowsiness, so needs to be used sensibly. It has also been used as a relaxant in cases of nervous colic.

Witch Hazel *(Hamamelis virginiana)*

Many households have a bottle of witch hazel in the medicine cabinet. This contains volatile oil and ethyl alcohol, but the shrub also contains tannin, saponin and organic acids. Due to its astringent properties it is used to treat sprains, insect bites and bruises. It can be applied as a poultice.

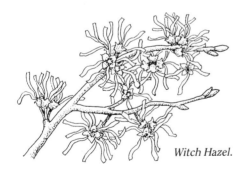

Witch Hazel.

Yarrow *(Achillea millefolium)*

Also known as milfoil, this tiny herb is a stimulant and diaphoretic useful in the treatment of heavy chest colds and 'flu. It contains achilleine, resin, gum and organic compounds, iron and sulphur. Additionally it is used as an astringent to aid bruises, and to help check blood flow from wounds. It can be applied as a poultice.

CASE HISTORY

PRINCESS: 16.2 hh showjumping mare, 6 years old. This horse is a good jumper at home but, unfortunately, she does not cope well with travelling and all the hustle and bustle of competitions. It was decided that she should be put on a calmative supplement, with ingredients that included chamomile, chicory and dandelion.

She had been on the supplement for two weeks prior to a major showjumping event. The journey there took three hours and the weather conditions were terrible, but the mare seemed to be coping remarkably well. She was calm when being unloaded and, even though the wind was howling, she did not spook and prance about in the collecting ring, as she had done on previous occasions.

When the mare went in to jump the wind was worse than ever and, just as she took off at the first fence, a sudden gust blew it down in front of her. She jumped aside steadily and stood like an old campaigner while the fence was erected again. She then proceeded around the course and jumped clear. She went on to finish a commendable third in the competition.

She remained in control of herself while travelling home and has not reverted to her old nervous behaviour since. She competes regularly and has notched up a fair amount of prize money in the two years she has been on the herbal supplement.

Herb Groups

Many herbs have a similar action and can be grouped accordingly.

Alteratives are used as an overall treatment for the beneficial alteration of a horse's condition. They are often known as blood cleansers and their use results in enhanced vigour and well-being which they accomplish by gradually restoring proper activity and balance of the body as a whole. Examples of alteratives include Plaintain, Dandelion, Fenugreek, Flax, Linseed.

Anodynes are beneficial in easing pain. Examples are Devil's Claw, Mugwort, Hops.

Antiseptics are herbs that prevent putrefaction. Chamomile, Rose hips, Rue and Southernwood are all antiseptics.

Anthelmintics act against intestinal worms. Garlic and Mint are included in this group.

Aperients have laxative properties. They have a gentle effect on the bowels which helps to ensure proper function. Examples are Linseed oil and Kelp.

Astringents contain tannins. They are used when a reduction in discharges is desirable as they cause contraction of body tissues. Sage, Thyme, Witch Hazel and Wild Geranium are all astringents.

Bitters, as their name suggests, are bitter-tasting herbs. They are used as a tonic to arouse the horse's digestive system. When the horse's taste buds detect the bitterness the brain sends a warning message to the digestive system which stimulates its action. Bitters include Chicory and Golden Rod.

Demulcents have a high mucilage content which is beneficial in the treatment of inflamed mucous

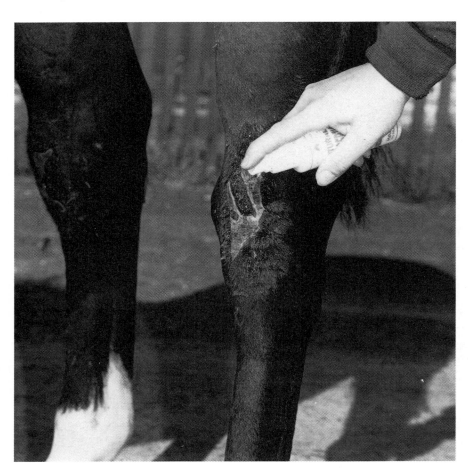

Antiseptic herbs are often included in convenient 'natural' wound sprays.

membranes. In general their effect is a soothing and calming one. Examples are Arnica, Eyebright, Marigold and Pennyroyal.

Diuretics increase the quantity and flow of urine. This is beneficial in disposing of an excess of fluid. Examples are Horseradish and Parsley.

Expectorants help to rid the lungs and throat of a build-up of excess mucus. This group includes Coltsfoot, Eucalyptus and Mint.

Nervines affect the nervous system and can alter its activity, either to arouse it or to calm it. It depends on what particular herb is used and what condition is being suffered as to which effect the nervines will have. Included in this group are the herbs Hyssop, Chamomile, Rosemary, Valerian and Red Clover.

Tonics include any herbs that have an ability to balance and sustain the body in such a way that ill health can be opposed – for example, Fenugreek, Linseed, Kelp, Nettle, Raspberry and Red Clover. A tonic, if used regularly, is said to add a special 'bloom' to the horse's condition.

Vulneraries are very beneficial in the first aid kit as they help to stimulate healing of injuries and lesions. This group includes Comfrey, Eyebright, Horseradish and Marigold.

THE PREPARATION OF HERBAL TREATMENTS

Infusions

A tea bag could technically be called an infusion sachet. Infusions are made by quickly pouring boiling water on previously prepared herbs. The mixture is allowed to stand for about 15 minutes, stirring frequently. It can be strained or not, depending on what it is going to be used for. Use 30 g (1 oz) of dried herbs or 70 g (2½ oz) of fresh herbs, to 300 ml (½ pt) of boiling water.

Decoctions

These are herbs which have been cut, ground up or bruised and covered with cold fresh water. This

Preparing an infusion by pouring boiling water over prepared herbs.

mixture is then boiled for half an hour, allowed to cool and then strained through a fine mesh. This method is normally used when the herb is unsuitable to make as an infusion. In general, use 30 g (1 oz) of dried herbs to 600 ml (1 pt) of water. With fresh herbs, use 70 g to 600 ml (2½ oz to 1 pt).

Solid extracts

Firstly make a strong infusion of the chosen herbs. Then evaporate over a low heat until a heavy consistency is achieved.

Tinctures

Tinctures are made with diluted or pure spirits of wine. It is necessary to prepare a tincture from herbs which become ineffective when heated, or for those herbs which are not responsive to treatment by water. For each 600 ml (1 pt) use 30–60 g (1–2 oz) of dried herbs or 60–120 g (2–4 oz) of fresh ones.

Poultice

When preparing a poultice use either fresh chopped herbs or dried herbs, dampened with hot water. The poultice is prepared in layers and the materials need to be large enough to cover the injury and to leave room for secure bandaging.

You will need a large plate, a square of polythene, a square of gamgee, the herbs, a kettle of boiling water and a clean bandage. Place the polythene on the large plate; lay the gamgee on top and add herbs sufficient to cover the affected area. Pour on the hot water and allow to soak. When you can bear the temperature with your fingers, squeeze out the excess water. Apply directly to the affected area and bandage with even pressure. Do not leave in place for more than eight hours, although a fresh poultice can be applied after another eight hours if necessary.

Plant oils

These can be obtained either by a method of extraction or by distillation. To distil, firstly boil the roots and stems of the herb for several hours, collecting the steam in another container. When this cools the essential oil will separate from the water and can easily be skimmed off and kept in a small bottle ready for use.

Extraction is used when the herb required is not amenable to treatment by water, or it becomes useless when heated. A solvent, usually alcohol, is continuously run through the plant material and collected in a still. After distillation, a mixture of waxes and essential oils is left in a solid lump.

Poultices can be made from fresh chopped or dried herbs, or they can be bought ready prepared.

Herbal fly repellent.

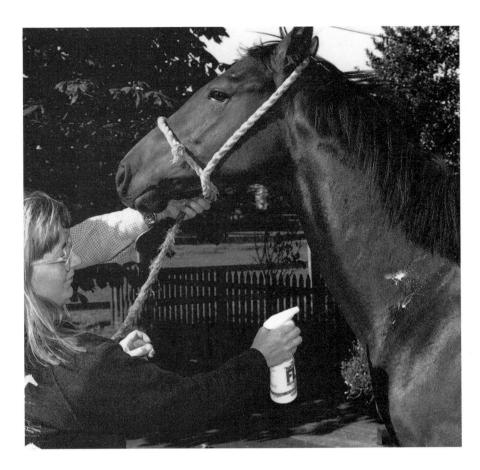

READY-MADE HERBAL REMEDIES

Many herbal companies now produce herbal remedies as well as herbal feed supplements. The range is growing rapidly and includes such products as antiseptic and massage sprays, creams, hoof dressings and shampoo. However, there is much satisfaction to be derived from treating your horse successfully with a preparation made by your own efforts and every horse owner will benefit from at least trying it before relying on bought preparations.

Herbal hoof dressings.

9 HOMOEOPATHY

Many people regard herbalism and homoeopathy as one and the same thing, but the two are separate treatments with differing principles. Homoeopathy is a therapy where drugs capable of causing disease in a healthy individual are given in minute doses to stimulate the body's own defences.

Homoeopathy works on the principle that 'like can cure like', with a conviction that substances which cause symptoms in a healthy body can be used to cure them in an unhealthy body. The principle is epitomized in the Latin maxim *'similila similibus curentur'*. By pairing the symptoms presented by a sick individual with the known toxic effects produced by a particular substance, that same substance, in a much diluted form, is used as a treatment.

The homoeopathic principle was discovered over 200 years ago by Samuel Hahnemann, a German physician, and is the basis for all homoeopathic treatments in use today. His first experiment involved Peruvian bark, from which quinine originates. He found that if a healthy person took Peruvian bark then they developed symptoms similar to those of malaria, a disease which is treated with quinine. He then went on to test many other natural substances – animal, mineral and vegetable – and found that they produced symptoms in the healthy body, which they could cure in a diseased body.

As a result, one of the principles of homoeopathy is that it is not necessary to have an exact diagnosis to treat ill health, as symptoms denote the result of the body fighting the disease, not that they are caused by the disease. Therefore, substances which can stimulate the symptoms are administered to the individual, so that they quicken the body's response to fight the disease.

Homoeopathic medicines, known as remedies, are selected for each individual case, depending on the symptom shown.

All remedies are diluted down to minute fractions of the original source, and the more dilute a substance, the more effective it is. Thus homoeopathy is a safe system of treatment which can be used without any fear of doping a horse. This is extremely beneficial to competition horses as there are no side effects and no residues are left to show up in drugs tests. Homoeopathic treatments can be used in place of conventional drugs such as bute and steroids. Some horses may be allergic to certain conventional drugs and in such cases a homoeopathic remedy is a good alternative.

A good homoeopath will know what to use in place of conventional drugs and, with no side effects, homoeopathic remedies can often control or even cure cases which were thought to be incurable.

WHAT REMEDY?

There are no hard and fast rules as to what homoeopathic remedy should be given for a particular problem. Two horses with the same condition may be given different remedies. They will often show different symptoms and so have different homoeopathic needs. The individual make-up of the horse must also be considered: for the same illness a highly strung, quick-tempered horse may receive a different remedy from that chosen for the docile, good tempered horse.

To understand this principle, let us take as an example arthritis, diagnosed in two horses.

Horse A appears to be in quite a lot of pain when the weather is damp and stiffens up after rest. When he receives mild exercise he appears to loosen up and receive some relief from the pain. The symptoms are more apparent in cold weather. The homoeopath decides to give this horse the homoeopathic remedy *Rhus toxidendron 1m*. He receives this potency once a day for a week, after which an improvement is observed. To relieve the pain and stiffness on a daily basis, the horse is put on to a routine dose of *30c* once a day.

Horse B appears to be better after resting but stiff and in pain when exercised. A gentle pressure massage over the joints seems to relieve the stiffness and pain. The homoeopath decides that *Bryonia 200c* is more suitable for this case and advises the owner to give this dose to the horse once or perhaps twice a day if needed.

Homoeopathic treatments are now being used for a wide variety of conditions with impressive results. As the principle is to exploit the body's own natural power to treat disease, the important thing is to match the right substance with the correct symptoms. It is not a simple process and with over 2,000 remedies to choose from it takes great skill and knowledge to select the appropriate remedy. While there is an extensive homoeopathic reference work – the *Materia Medica* (originally intended for humans) – it is not something which can be learned through text books as every horse presents individual symptoms for similar conditions. Immense practical experience is necessary.

Homoeopathic medicine is not a way of saving money by dispensing with the services of veterinary surgeons, nor does it necessarily replace conventional treatment, especially if surgery is indicated. To derive the most benefit from homoeopathic medicine, particularly in all but the most minor ailments, you should involve your own veterinary surgeon and ask that he liaises with, and requests a visit from, a recognized equine homoeopath. This will ensure that you are all working together for the good of your horse.

WHAT TO EXPECT FROM HOMOEOPATHIC TREATMENT

Your first dealings with a homoeopathic veterinary surgeon will probably be quite a welcome surprise. Firstly he will endeavour to involve you as much as possible and secondly he will take time to get to know you and your horse. It is necessary that he knows everything that is occurring with your horse

CASE HISTORIES

ROCKY: 15.3 hh bay gelding, 3-year-old racehorse. This horse often pulled up with a bleeding nose after races. The veterinary surgeon diagnosed epistaxis (another name for nose bleeds). As the trainer wanted the horse to be treated without any fear of using banned drugs, he called in a homoeopath. The homoeopath observed one of these nosebleeds after a race and, as the blood was bright red, was satisfied that the horse did not have a diseased condition but that the nose bleeds were simply as a result of over-exertion.

On completion of the race the horse was treated with *Aconitum napellus 6c*. He was then given three further doses every hour. The bleeding stopped rapidly, and although the horse still has nose bleeds from time to time they are far less frequent and the same treatment soon remedies the situation. The horse is still racing.

BUBBLES: 14.2, 3-year-old, unbroken pony. This pony started to become irritable and bad-tempered for no apparent reason. Nothing had altered in the way the pony was kept to bring about this sudden change, but the vet suggested it might be a teething problem. *Chamomilla x 30* was given and within 48 hours the pony had settled down and reverted to her normal happy self.

if he is to be able to treat him as whole and remove the barriers to recovery.

Homoeopathic treatment, like so many other natural therapies is all about treating the horse as a whole. Homoeopaths believe that the body has an innate power to heal itself, and they are just lifting the restrictions which are causing ill-health. In order to remove these barriers the homoeopath will ask questions about your horse's medical history, his background, his character, his behaviour, his routine and normal environment and about the work he has been doing and how the illness has progressed. Was it sudden, or has it been a gradual process, for example? Even though your horse may have been referred from another vet, who may have already given a diagnosis, the homoeopath will re-examine the horse, because things that may seem trivial to you or your conventional vet may be important in terms of homoeopathy. Only when he is satisfied with the information given and his own examination will he decide upon an appropriate form of treatment. This may be homoeopathy – to the exclusion of all other therapies, or it may be a combination of therapies – homoeopathy and chiropractic, for instance.

ADMINISTERING HOMOEOPATHIC TREATMENTS

Homoeopathic treatments come in tablets, creams, granules, pills, triturations, powders and liquids. They can be bought from many chemists and health food stores, although you need to be sure that you are using the right preparation for the right symptoms. While it is sensible to involve a homoeopathic specialist in any serious or recurring illness, you can build up a first-aid kit of homoeopathic remedies for use in emergencies or very mild conditions. Again, if in doubt always check with a specialist.

The strength of a particular remedy is denoted by a centesimal scale number: the higher the number, the more dilute a substance and so the more potent it is. The most commonly used potencies are 6, 12, 30 and 200. For example, one drop of a substance

with a potency of 6c will have had 99 drops of water added. One drop of the resulting solution is then mixed with another 99 drops of water. This is repeated until it has been accomplished six times, so you can see that we are talking about very dilute substances indeed.

The use of such dilute substances is a very hard principle to understand if traditionally you have been accustomed to using more of something if the current dose is not working. However, instead of suppressing symptoms, as in conventional medicine, homoeopathic remedies aid the healing process by stimulating the body's own natural defence mechanisms. It is only because homoeopathic remedies are used in such dilutions that a vital reaction and thus stimulation of the affected tissue is produced.

Homoeopathic remedies are more usually available in tablet form. This can pose a problem for the horse owner as the tablets are supposed to be dissolved under the tongue. This is a little difficult to convey to the horse, who is likely to want to spit it

Homoeopathic treatments are available in cream form.

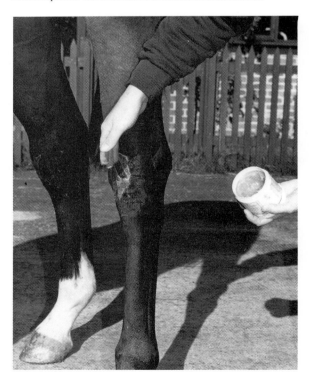

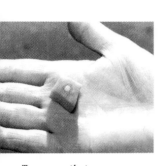

To ensure that a homoeopathic remedy is accepted, a small hole can be gouged out of a carrot cube and the tablet popped in.

The carrot cube is then simply offered to the horse.

out. Additionally the tablet should not be touched by the human hand, so how do you go about it?

If you are fairly confident that you will be able to hold your horse's head still you can slip a tablet under your horse's tongue and hold his head high until the tablet has had time to dissolve. This will provide the best possible means for the tablet to work quickly as it will then be absorbed through the buccas mucosa in the mouth which ensures swift absorption into the system.

The headshy horse will pose more problems and it may prove impossible to place the tablet under the tongue for the desired time. For the difficult horse it is far better to get the tablet into the system than to not get it in at all. A small hole can be gouged out of a small square of carrot and the tablet popped in. The carrot is then offered to the horse who will eat it without suspicion. The treatment will simply take longer to work as it will be delayed by going through the digestive system.

It is also possible to buy homoeopathic remedies in a water-based solution which is administered from a dropper, straight into the mouth, however they are more difficult to obtain in this form.

Some remedies need to be given every 10 or 15 minutes while others are used over a longer period, perhaps twice or three times daily. The frequency of dosage should be adhered to strictly, since this is more important than the amount of tablets given.

Homoeopathic treatments are not meant for long term use, unless directed by the specialist. As soon as an improvement is shown then the treatment should be ceased otherwise a recurrence of the original symptoms may arise, or else new ones may present themselves.

While it is impossible to give a list of what remedies can be used for what conditions, because of the individualization of treatment, the following list gives remedies that have been used in the majority of cases for given conditions. The advice of a specialist should be obtained for all but the most minor of ailments.

Arthritis:	**Apis** in the early stages. **Rhus Tox** where the horse seems in more pain after rest. **Bryonia** when the horse seems better after rest.
Bee stings:	**Apis.**
Conjunctivitis:	**Aconite** at the onset. **Euphrasia** diluted tincture is used to flush out the eye. **Hypericum** and **Calendula** lotion can also be used to clear eye discharge.
Colic:	**Nux vomica** at the onset. **Aconite** in the early stages **Colocynthis** for spasmodic colic. The potency should be increased for severe cases. **Colchicum** for flatulent colic.
Dehydration:	**China.**
Diarrhoea:	**Arsenicum** album. **China** when loss of a large amount of fluid has occurred as a result of the diarrhoea. **Lycopodium** where a problem with the liver is thought to be the cause. **Mercuritus** where the dung is slimy. **Arsenicum** where the dung is watery and light coloured. **Podophyllum** for established, recurring cases.
Fever:	**Aconite** in the early stages **Belladonna** where there is a bounding pulse, nervous excitability and dilated pupils.
Influenza:	**Aconite** in the initial stages. **Belladonna** where there is a sudden high fever. **Gelsemium** where there is muscle weakness and incoordination. **Phosphorus** when the eyes are glazed.
Insect bites:	**Ledum.**
Muscle strain:	**Arnica** internally and as a topical agent.
Navicular:	**Bryonia** for the early acute inflammatory stage. **Calcarea fluorica** for a developing condition. **Silicea** for an established condition. **Brucella abortus** nosode given routinely along with other remedies.
Nerve injuries:	**Hypericum** to relieve pain.
Nervous tension:	**Aconite** and **Gelsemium.**
Oedema and swelling:	**Apis.**
Open wounds:	**Calendula** given orally

and a tincture applied as a topical agent.

Calendula and Hypericum lotion (in equal parts) will aid healing.

Arnica (but note that Arnica should never be used topically for open wounds).

Pregnancy: Arnica before, during and after birth.

Puncture wounds: Hypericum tincture, often combined with Calendula, can be used to flush out the wound. Once healing begins Hypericum, or combined Hypericum and Calendula ointment can be used.

Ledum is especially useful where the wound does not bleed and combined with Hypericum helps to prevent tetanus.

Apis can be used where swelling is present.

Ringworm: Bacillinum where rough dry skin is present.

Hydrocotyle where there are scaly lesions.

Shock: Aconite.
Arnica.

Spinal injuries: Hypericum quickly relieves pain.

Stiffness: Arnica.

Surgery: Arnica before and after surgery.

Tendon strain: Ruta. Can be combined with Arnica for associated tendon and soft tissue damage.

Rhus tox for general tendon inflammation.

Silicea for chronic cases.

Warts: Thuja. Thuja tincture can also be applied topically.

CASE HISTORIES

WILLIAM: 16.2 chestnut gelding, 8-year-old event horse. This horse was found very poorly in his box one morning in the summer after a strenuous day's eventing. His coat was 'stary' and his skin dry and shrunken. His eye was sunken and he had an insatiable thirst. He was very weak and reluctant to walk out of his box. On examination his heart rate was increased and his blood pressure lower than normal. Dehydration was diagnosed.

The horse needed something to restore his strength and promote a return to his normal physiological condition. *China off. 30c* was given three times a day for three days. On re-examination the horse had returned to normal.

SAILOR: 15.2 grey gelding, 6 years old, show horse. This horse reacted badly to his yearly tetanus injections. At first the owner thought that he was just suffering from mild after-effects, but on examination the veterinary surgeon detected an allergy to tetanus injections.

Hypericum was administered instead by a homoeopath, with no side effects. The horse receives his yearly dose of *Hypericum* to protect against tetanus and the horse has a certificate to prove he has received such protection.

10 BACK TO WORK

No alternative method of training or form of preventive healthcare is a complete system in itself. At first, certain alternatives can be used to put the horse back on the road to recovery, but ultimately there will come a time when normal ridden work should recommence. This is in order to develop the horse further both physically and mentally. The principles of alternative training and complementary therapies can be maintained – that is, to continue to regard the horse as a whole being. Without a sound mind he cannot reach peak performance; without a sound body his performance will be less than his best.

Horses trained for high performance are expected to jump higher, gallop faster and stay the distance better than their equine opponents. It is obvious

In remedial work long-reining is used as a link between other remedial therapies and ridden work.

that at some stage the horse has to experience jumping high, galloping fast and enduring long rides. Only then can he hope to compete well in the discipline for which his owner has aimed him.

There are no 'wonder' treatments and there are no short cuts to producing elite equine athletes. We must never forget that every horse is an individual and that if he does not have the natural ability to be a top performer, then no amount of alternative training will make him into one.

The same goes for complementary treatments. They may be able to help where conventional medicine has failed, but they will never be able to produce a miracle cure. Recovery is a process which involves the natural healing powers of the horse. As

described throughout this book, complementary therapies in the main are designed to provide the best possible environment for natural healing to take place. The aim is to effect a remedy for the problem, not merely to mask it with drugs so that the horse can still compete. In some cases, though, the 'alternative' will not be able to offer help: for instance, surgery may be necessary in a life-threatening condition and in such a case no amount of holistic care will solve the problem.

THE ROAD TO RECOVERY

Inevitably then, the natural progression of healing brings a time when the alternative fitness prog-ramme has to come to an end. The horse will need to adjust to a new regime, which is usually his former one. However, some things can carry on, such as the feeding of herbal supplements and the occasional use of swimming or treadmill exercise as a change from conventional exercise.

The next step after alternative exercise is re-education to conventional exercise, firstly by loose schooling and long-reining and ultimately by riding. Lungeing is not particularly useful when re-educating the horse, especially when re-educating movement after injury. Firstly the horse is always working on a bend and secondly lungeing puts strain on joints, which is the very thing that is not wanted.

The first task is to get the horse working efficiently, with all limbs in harmony. Inefficient movement and lack of coordination within the gaits is a common cause of injury, especially to the tendons. In order to conserve energy and oxygen consumption the horse has inherent gears in which he travels with ease. From a foal he will have established an optimum cruising speed within each gait, at which it is most comfortable and efficient for him to travel.

When you ask your horse to 'speed up', if left to his own devices he will change gait naturally when he reaches the appropriate speed. This is in order to conserve energy. If you expect your horse to retain the gait, but at a higher speed, asking for an extended trot rather than a canter for example, his energy consumption jumps considerably. It also

Rehabilitation uses gymnastic exercises to help rectify wayward movement. (a) Trotting poles evenly spaced; (b) one end of each pole is raised from left to right to encourage the horse to lift his limbs consciously and evenly; (c) side view of (b); (d) the beginning of a small jumping grid to help produce a supple outline.

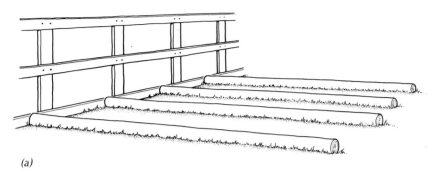

(a)

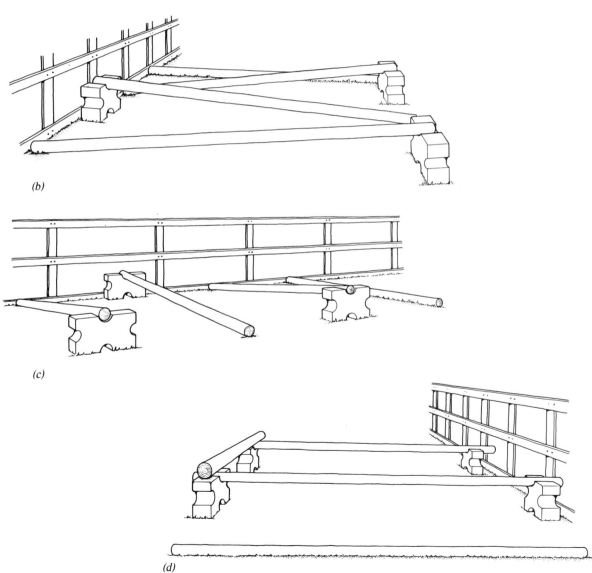

(b)

(c)

(d)

Rehabilitation uses gymnastic exercises over poles and small grids to achieve a good, supple outline which produces agile and regular paces.

takes more energy to keep a horse in a particular gait at a lower speed, asking him to remain in canter when naturally he would break into a trot, for example. It is therefore just as tiring for a horse to go too slowly within a gait as too fast.

It is important, then, to go slowly and only ask for more complicated movements when you are sure the horse is fit enough to take the strain. Remember that too much, too soon, ruins horses – little and often is the key.

LOOSE SCHOOLING

During loose schooling after a lay-off from work, you can reintroduce the horse to all of his previous activities as soon as he is physically and mentally ready for them. Loose schooling also gives a good indication of how well the horse has recovered. He may be a little tentative at first, but as soon as he regains his confidence he should be happy and willing to work.

The jumping horse can be jumped without a rider on his back. This is beneficial when establishing full recovery before ridden work commences. If the horse shows signs of pecking or coming up short, then he needs more time before being ridden.

LONG-REINING

Long-reining is far more effective and useful than lungeing. In remedial work it is usually used as a link between other remedial therapy (such as hydroexercise) and normal ridden work. The aim is to rebuild weak muscles, strengthening their power, and to achieve a balanced and flexible outline, which lessens the likelihood of breakdown when ridden work commences after a prolonged lay-off.

There are various methods of long-reining, each originating from different countries. The English method is probably the most suited to the purpose of rehabilitation, as the horse is allowed a longer and more free outline. Once the horse is back to normal, other methods can be used to achieve the aims of a specific discipline.

Rehabilitation work differs from that of initial training with long reins. The purpose of initial training is to prepare the horse for ridden work. Rehabilitation also prepares the horse to resume ridden work but it has a further purpose of rectifying wayward movement, which is often a result of injury. Rehabilitation uses gymnastic exercises to achieve a good, supple outline which produces agile and regular paces. Poles and small grids are used to help attain even movement as the horse has to make a conscious effort to place his limbs correctly, or he will keep knocking the poles. A spin-off of such work is an even tempo, which may be better than that which the horse had prior to the injury.

If you do not know how to arrange the poles and grids, ask your horse's physiotherapist to explain how to set them up to obtain the most benefit for your particular horse.

RIDDEN WORK

Ridden work completes the full circle of recovery from injury or illness, through complementary therapies and alternative training to rehabilitation. It is often the last step in what may have been a long road back to complete health.

You should not expect simply to start back where you left off however, as the horse will not be the same as he was just before the injury occurred. His body will have gone through a tremendous alteration. He will have suffered pain and perhaps the loss of use of one or more of his limbs, so that his confidence will have suffered a severe blow. The only way to proceed is cautiously, taking the horse right back to basics. If you jump straight on and fire him up you may undo all the good that has been achieved in the preceding months.

Firstly the horse will have to become accustomed to carrying a rider again, so plenty of slow walking around the countryside will be of great help. It will also help to re-establish the bond between horse and rider. Once the horse shows signs of coping with a rider, then you can begin fitness training, ensuring

Left: Ridden work completes the full circle of recovery from injury to rehabilitation.

Right: Plenty of slow walking around the countryside with a companion will be of great benefit.

that none of the contributory factors which caused the injury in the first place are present. If the saddle pinches, have it fixed or buy a new one; if you have discovered that your riding position contributed in any way to the injury then take lessons from a good instructor and make a huge conscious effort to improve your own riding ability. A performance horse can only achieve his best if he is part of a skilful combination.

Horse Walkers

Many yards now have a horse walker and its benefits are many and varied. Not only does it allow horses to be exercised when there is no time to ride them, or no rider available, but it is also useful as a fitness and therapeutic aid.

As described in Chapter 2, the early stages of fitness training require much walking to be done. This can be time-consuming for the busy rider who would much rather be working on another horse and it can also become very boring. Putting the horse in the horse walker frees the rider for more demanding ridden work. It also imposes less strain on the horse's flabby muscles and tendons than if he were delegated to some groom's lungeing session.

Once the horse is ready for more demanding work, the horse walker can also provide a warm up to exercise, or a cool down after strenuous work, which helps to prevent muscle damage.

Horse walkers can also be used with less possibility of strain for a convalescing or young horse, as they afford slow, gentle exercise. A convalescing horse would traditionally have to be walked out in-hand at least twice a day, so time saving is another benefit of these devices.

The physiotherapist can often maintain the fitness of an injured horse by using a walker. Horses with a back complaint or some other injury preventing ridden exercise, can be walked for a hour or so a day to maintain general muscle tone and fitness. The physiotherapist can also combine the use of the walker with other remedial work to devise a programme to benefit each horse individually.

Many horse walkers have varying speeds which can be regulated to a particular pace or an individual

The best type of horsewalkers are those where the horse can be left loose within the specially designed cage.

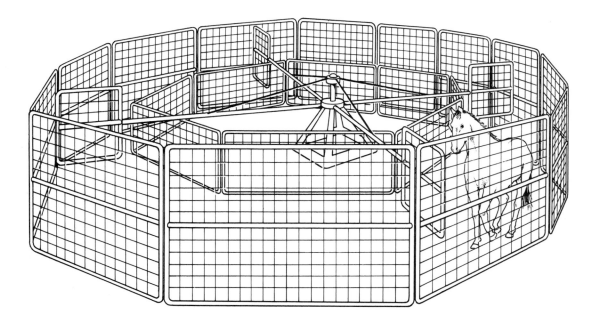

horse's stride. Most horses seem to accept the horse walker quite readily. The biggest problem is preventing boredom and as a result the lazy horse may decide to stop. Most walkers have a safety mechanism which stops the walker if it meets with undue resistance, therefore the lazy horse may soon learn that he can stop the machine if he wants to, which can be a drawback. Some owners prefer to tie their horses on to the walker, but the best results (and the safest) are obtained by leaving the horse loose within the specially designed cage.

To prevent boredom the horse should be allowed periods out at grass, combined with other forms of passive exercise if possible, so that he is not confined to stable and horse walker day in, day out.

PREVENTION IS BETTER THAN CURE!

While carrying out your rehabilitation programme remember your new found knowledge. Are you satisfying your horse's nutritional needs? Is your blacksmith shoeing him well? Is your horse coping with his workload? Is he enthusiastic? Does he have enough freedom...?

As you can see, re-education is in fact a system. The horse's whole environment needs to be examined and improvements made as a result. By standing back and taking a good look at the overall picture, you can often pinpoint weaknesses and rectify them to prevent further problems.

Whenever your horse competes, he will suffer negligible injury to his soft tissues no matter how well developed he is at the time. This is not a problem if each time he competes he receives care that will enable repair of the damage before he competes again. If such small injuries are ignored, because they are thought to be of little consequence, they will build up until one day the horse suffers quite a significant injury, which may put him totally out of action.

Your horse may not be lame, but you should be aware if he is suffering pain. Constant effort is required to keep a performance horse in tip top condition, and conscientious owners will be sure to monitor their horses with the utmost care and attention at all times.

BACK TO WORK

How well does the healthy, alternatively trained horse do in competition? This obviously depends on why the horse was laid off, how long recovery took and the extent of recovery. Sometimes horses do not fully recover; a sprained tendon will always be a weak link, for example. However, there are some interesting comparisons between horses treated conventionally and those which have received alternative care. It has been suggested by various studies, on both humans and horses, that the quality of repair offered by physiotherapy machines is better than that of conventional treatment – which all too often is rest. So when treated with physiotherapy the horse may be less likely to breakdown.

An alternatively trained horse may also be mentally more stable than a traditionally trained counterpart. His routine will have been demanding and varied, which helps to build enthusiasm and a willingness to 'do the job'. It is likely that the conventionally cared for horse is just as able to perform to maximum potential as the alternatively trained one, but the difference is plain when a weakness arises.

An old injury is always a weak link. It may stand up to many more years of work if it is nurtured but inevitably it has a readier breaking point than an uninjured structure. If the quality of repair has been good, such as is often achieved with physiotherapy, this breaking point will be nearer to that of an uninjured structure and so breakdown is less likely.

ADAPTATION

It is important to understand how to retrain an injured part to make it stronger. Adaptation is the key, but it takes patience and skill. You need to stress the weak link so that it 'learns' to cope, but not to such an extent that it breaks down. The stress needs to be built up gradually until the horse is able to perform without risk. The jumping horse will start by jumping small fences, their height increasing as he confirms his ability to cope. Similarly the dressage horse will be asked to perform increasingly difficult movements to confirm his stage of recovery.

This is measured by the horse not showing any symptoms from the injury or condition suffered. When the horse can perform as well as prior to injury, without any sign of pain or stress, then he is said to be fully recovered. If your horse does not show signs of a full recovery, you may have to face the fact that he has sustained permanent injury which will always have an effect on his ability.

Conventional treatment and training seem only to restore the horse to his former condition, which may have been less than ideal anyway. The alternative can have a higher success rate, because the horse is treated as a whole being, and no part of his health or fitness gets overlooked.

As stated there are no miracles. This book does not intend to present complementary therapies and alternative fitness methods as miracle cures. They simply provide another option for the horse owner which, if sampled, may well unlock the door to the horse's future.

Alternative therapies provide another option which may well unlock the door to a horse's future.

USEFUL ADDRESSES

UK

Animal Health Trust
Balaton Lodge
Snailwell Road
PO Box 5
Newmarket
Suffolk CB8 7DW

Argyll Herbalists
The Natural Healing Centre
Coombe Valley
Winscombe
Somerset BS25 1DA

Association of British Veterinary
    Acupuncture
East Park Cottage
Handcross
West Sussex
RH17 6BD

Association of Chartered Physiotherapists
    in Animal Therapy
7 Wellfield Road
Culcheth
Warrington
Cheshire WA3 4JR

BBA Equine Hydroexercise
The Hastings Centre
The Watercourse
Exeter Road
Newmarket
Suffolk

British Association of Homoeopathic
    Veterinary Surgeons
Chinham House
Stanford-in-the-Vale
Faringdon
Oxon SN7 8NQ

British Homoeopathic Association
27a Devonshire Street
London
W1N 1RJ

Complete Animal Therapy (CAT)
8 Church Terrace
Cheveley
Newmarket
Suffolk
CD8 9DH

Feedmark
St Cross
Harleston
Norfolk PI20 0NY

Hilton Herbs
Victoria Farm
Brookwood
Surrey GU24 0AQ

Horse and Rider Health Centre
Milton Keynes Eventing Centre
Malt Mill Farm
Hanslope
Bucks MK19 7HQ

McTimoney Chiropractic
The Institute of Pure Chiropractic
14 Park End Street
Oxford
OX1 1HH

McTimoney Chiropractic
The Oxford McTimoney Chiropractic Clinic
40 North Hinskey Lane
Botley
Oxford OX22 0LY

Mary M Bromiley
(Equine physiotherapist)
Downs House
Baydon
Nr Marlborough
Wilts SN8 2JS

National Association of
    Animal Therapists
c/o Animal Therapy Limited
Tyringham Hall
Cuddington
Aylesbury
Buckinghamshire HP18 0AS

National Association of
    Medical Herbalists
41 Hatherley Road
Winchester
Hampshire SO22 6RR

Northern Equine Therapy Centre
Beautry House
Rathmell
Settle
North Yorkshire BD24 0LA

Royal College of Veterinary Surgeons
32 Belgrave Square
London
SW1X 8QP

USA and Canada

American Veterinary Chiropractic Assn.
PO Box 249
Port Byron
IL 61275

BHI (Homoeopathic)
11600 Cochiti South East
Albuquerque
NM 87123

International Veterinary
  Acupuncture Society
2140 Conestoga Road
Chester Springs
PA 19425

Meadowbrook Herb Garden
93 Kingstown Road
Wyoming
RI 02898

Medical Equipment Sales and Service
(Bradley T Wilhelm)
29885 Second Street
Lake Elsinore
CA 92330

Standard Homoeopathic
210 W. 131st Street
Box 61067
Los Angeles
CA 90061

World-Wide Herb Limited
11 Sainte Catherine Street East
Montreal 129
Canada

FURTHER READING

Britton, Vanessa *Training the Young Horse*, Batsford, 1994

Bromiley, Mary *Equine Injury and Therapy*, Blackwell Scientific Publications, 1993

Clayton, Hilary *Conditioning Sport Horses*, Sport Horse Publications, 1991

Gray, Peter *Soundness in the Horse*, J. A. Allen, 1993

Hodges, Jo and Pilliner, Sarah *The Equine Athlete*, Blackwell Scientific Publications, 1991

Holderness-Roddam, Jane *Fitness for Horse and Rider*, David and Charles, 1993

Macleod, George *The Treatment of Horses by Homoeopathy*, The C W Daniel Co. Ltd., 7th impression 1991

Meagher, Jack *Beating Muscle Injuries for Horses*, J. A. Allen, 1986

Pilliner, Sarah *Getting Horses Fit*, Blackwell Scientific Publications, 1993

Porter, Mimi *Equine Sports Therapy*, Veterinary Data, 1990

Smythe, R. H. *Horse Structure and Movement*, J. A. Allen, 1993

Snader, Meredith; Willoughby, Sharon; Khalsa, Deva Kaur; Denega, Craig and Basko, Ihor John *Healing Your Horse, Alternative Therapies*, Howell Book House, 1993

Snow, D. H. and Vogel C. J. *Equine Fitness*, David and Charles, 1987

Tellington Jones, L. and Bruns, Ursula *An Introduction to the Tellington Jones Equine Awareness Method*, Breakthrough Publications, New York 1990

Westermayer, Erwin *The Treatment of Horses by Acupuncture*, Health Science Press (J. A. Allen) 1979

Wilson, Gary L. and Mueller, Martha *The Equine Athlete*, Veterinary Learning Systems, 1982

Zidonis, Nancy; Soderberg, Mary and Pederson, Stacey *Equine Acupressure*, Equine Acupressure Inc, Colorado

GLOSSARY

Abrasion: area of broken skin.

Acupuncture: method of stimulating certain points on and within the body, usually with needles, to treat various conditions.

Acupuncture point: the point which is stimulated to cause an effect.

Acute: having a brief and relatively severe development.

Adaptation: process by which the horse, or part, learns to adjust and cope with a new external influence.

Adhesion: unnatural fusion of tissues.

Aerobic: where the presence of oxygen is essential.

Alternative fitness training: fitness methods, in contrast to conventional ones, where the horse is not ridden.

Alternative therapies: therapies which provide other options to conventional treatment.

Anaerobic functioning: where the presence of oxygen is not necessary.

Anaerobic metabolism: where a structure is working without oxygen.

Anaerobic threshold: the point at which anaerobic functioning takes over from aerobic functioning.

Anaesthesia: where consciousness or sensation is lost.

Anaesthetic: agent that produces partial or complete insensitivity to pain.

Analgesic: drug that gives relief from pain.

Anatomy: bodily structure of the horse and relationship of its parts.

Antibacterial: substance capable of killing bacteria.

Antibiotic: substance or drug which kills or prevents the spread of bacteria.

Antiseptic: substance or drug which prevents the decay of tissue by controlling the development of micro-organisms.

Asymmetry: lack of symmetry.

Articular: concerning joints.

Athletic ability: capability of the horse to perform as desired without undue stress.

Atrophy: the wasting away of a normally developed muscle, tissue or organ due to degeneration of cells or lack of use.

Blood tests: where a sample of blood is removed from a horse and tested in the laboratory for various reasons.

Blistering: the process of applying a substance to the skin which will produce inflammation, usually used to treat tendons and inflamed joints.

Bute: (phenylbutazone) painkilling drug.

Cardiac: concerning the heart.

Cardiovascular: involving the heart and blood vessels.

Chronic: a continued, long-term state.

Circulation: movement of blood or other fluid through vessels.

Circulatory system: that which employs the heart, blood, blood vessels, lymphatic vessels and lymph.

Cohesive property: tendency to remain united; that which keeps things together.

Collagen: the main protein of skin, bone, tendon, cartilage and connective tissue.

Complementary: that which works with or

corresponds with something else (the horse's natural healing powers, for instance).

Conditioning: pre-fitness work.

Contraindicated: that which is not advisable.

Contusion: an injury which occurs without breaking the skin, such as a bruise.

Conventional treatments: those which are traditionally used by veterinary surgeons (drugs, for example).

Cortisone: substance with an anti-inflammatory action.

Deficiency: a lack of something.

Dehydration: condition where too much fluid is lost from the body.

Deltoid: muscle of the shoulder.

Diagnosis: the identification of a disease or injury derived from tests, examinations and observations.

Dislocation: displacement of a part, usually a joint.

Dorsal: concerning the back.

Dysfunction: disturbance of an organ or function.

Effleurage: a type of massage technique.

Endorphins: pain relieving substances naturally produced by the nervous system.

Equine physiology: the study of the organs, tissues and metabolic function of the horse.

Faradism: treatment which uses a machine to produce a rhythm of contractions within a muscle.

Fast twitch: type of muscle which produces great power but for short periods.

Flexion: the act of bending or curving.

Fracture: breakage, especially of bone.

Friction: a type of massage stroke.

Gait: the way and sequence of the horse's movement.

Geriatric: relating to the older horse.

Glycogen: the body's chief carbohydrate storing substance.

Haematoma: a solid swelling or tumour formed by an accumulation of clotted blood within tissues.

Haemorrhage: bleeding, where blood leaks from the blood vessels.

Healthcare professionals: those trained to manage the health of horses through various means.

Herbalism: the practice of using herbs.

Holism: treating as a whole; not reducing to a sum of parts.

Homoeopathy: treatment of disease by the use of substances in minute doses, that in a healthy horse would produce symptoms like those of the disease.

H Wave: type of therapeutic machine used by a physiotherapist.

Hydroexercise: exercise which involves water.

Hydrostatic pressure: the equilibrium and pressure exerted by water.

Hydrotherapy: therapy which involves water.

Immune system: that which acts to protect against disease.

Inflammation: a reaction of the tissues when injured which results in redness, heat, swelling and pain.

Interval training: system of fitness training where the horse is exerted, allowed to partially recover and then exerted again.

Joints: the place where two or more bones meet.

Laceration: a wound which has torn the skin.

Lactic acid: a natural acid produced in muscle by anaerobic muscle metabolism.

Laser: high energy beam of intensive light concentrating heat and power at a close range.

Lesion: change in texture or structure due to injury.

Ligament: that which connects bones and cartilage.

Long-reining: a method of schooling the horse from the ground using two long reins.

Loose schooling: a method of schooling from the ground where the horse is loose and there is no physical link between horse and trainer.

Lumbar: of the back, especially concerning the loins.

Lymph: substance present in lymphatic vessels.

Lymphatic flow: the transportation of lymph around the lymphatic system.

Maintenance swimming: swimming to sustain a level of fitness, especially if the horse cannot be ridden.

Malnourished: undernourished, underfed.

Manipulation: manual examination and treatment of a part of the body using skilful techniques.

Massage: rubbing and kneading the muscles of the body to stimulate their action and relieve strain.

Meridian: energy course running along pathways of the body.

Metabolism: the sum of the horse's chemical and physical activity.

Muscle atrophy: wasting away of the muscle.

Musculoskeletal: made up of bones, joints, ligaments, muscles and tendons which together provide the propulsive force of the body.

Natural therapies: methods of healing by innate and instinctive means.

Nerves: pathways which carry messages to and from the brain.

Nervous system: that which coordinates the whole activity of the body.

Osteopath: specialist in treating and correcting imbalances of the skeleton.

Oedema: soft swellings that will depress when pressure is applied.

Palpation: feeling and examining with the hands.

Passive movements: gentle movements made by the handler to move limbs etc., rather than the horse moving them himself.

Pathological: concerning disease – the effects on tissue, body structures and organs.

Periosteum: thin tissue covering bones.

Petrissage: type of massage stroke.

Physiotherapy: the treatment of injury by mechanical and physical methods.

Poultice: hot or cold substance applied to an injury to relieve swelling and/or extract any foreign bodies.

Preventive treatment: treatment given in order to avoid illness and disease.

Prognosis: prediction of how something might progress or end.

Proliferation: to grow by multiplication causing, for instance, a rapid increase in cells.

Proud flesh: excessive tissue, causing a lump of external flesh.

Pulmonary: concerning the lungs.

Pulse: beat of the artery which can be felt with the hand, governed by the heart rate.

Pus: substance produced by inflammation which contains cells, bacteria and fluid.

Recovery rate: the speed at which a horse recovers to normality after exercise, determined by measuring the pulse and respiration.

Remedial work: work done to aid recovery.

Remodelling: the process which bone or other structure undergoes to reconstruct itself.

Respiration rate: the number of breaths within a minute.

Respiratory system: involving the lungs and airways.

Rupture: tissue which has torn or broken.

Sacroiliac: concerning the sacrum and ilium and related ligaments.

Scar tissue: the tissue which is still left after a wound has healed.

Slow twitch: muscles which contract slowly but which can endure lengthened work periods.

Spasm: fierce and unwilling contraction of muscle/s which causes pain.

Sprain: the result of abnormal stretching of a limb, usually causing partial or full ligament rupture.

Stamina: power of endurance.

Steroids: one of a large group of organic compounds with four carbon rings.

Strain: resulting from overwork to the horse's musculature.

Stress: forcibly exerted weight or pressure.

Subluxation: partial dislocation.

Tendon: cord which attaches muscle to bone.

TENS: (Transcutaneous Electrical Nerve Stimulators) type of therapeutic machine.

Therapy: the treatment of illness or injury.

Thermography: a method of recording the heat of body surfaces, usually used in diagnosing.

Thoracic: one of the vertebrae of the withers region.

Thorax: part between the withers and diaphragm.

TPR: temperature, pulse and respiration.

Trauma: wound, injury or extreme shock.

Treadmill: automatically controlled moving surface meant to take the weight of a horse.

Ultrasound: a machine emitting radiant energy with a frequency greater than 20,000 cycles per second, which is used by the physiotherapist.

Vaccine: substance administered to prevent infectious disease.

Vascular: full of vessels.

Veins: a vessel which carries de-oxygenated blood back to the heart.

Venous: concerning the veins.

Vertebrae: bones of the spinal column.

Vertebral column: bones which run from head to tail.

Water treadmill: treadmill which is enclosed in water so that the horse can be partially buoyant.

Water walks: places in which the horse can walk in water; can be either constructed or naturally occurring.

INDEX